BRACTON

AND

HIS RELATION TO THE ROMAN LAW.

A

CONTRIBUTION TO THE HISTORY OF THE ROMAN LAW
IN THE MIDDLE AGES.

BY

CARL GÜTERBOCK,

PROFESSOR OF LAW IN THE UNIVERSITY OF KŒNIGSBERG.

TRANSLATED BY

BRINTON COXE.

PHILADELPHIA:
J. B. LIPPINCOTT & CO.
1866.

[*Published by the Author's permission.*]

TRANSLATOR'S PREFACE.

Bracton's relation to the Roman law is one of the most interesting questions in historical jurisprudence. To an American or English lawyer it is, in fact, a fundamental question. Notwithstanding the great originality of the English law, it is manifest that the influence of the Roman law has affected it to an important extent. In order to ascertain accurately the nature and effect of that influence, it is first necessary to determine the position which Bracton, the father of our legal learning, bears to the Roman law. In this, as in other matters connected with the early history of the English law, Bracton is the most important authority. The period at which he wrote, his ability as a jurist, the richness of matter in his work, all combine to make it necessary to exhaust the sources of knowledge to be derived from him.

Bracton's relation to the Roman law has long been considered a question of much importance. In 1787 Mr. Reeves expressed the opinion that it should be thoroughly investigated by some competent jurist. Although a question constantly recurring, it, however, remained in England unsolved, and even so recent a writer as Professor Maine holds Bracton's relation to the Roman law to be among the most hopeless enigmas of jurisprudence. The investigation of Bracton's relation to the Roman law has, however, at length been undertaken by Dr. Güterbock, one of the superior judges of the Stadtgericht of Kœnigsberg, and Professor of Law in the University of that city; and the translator has felt that an English version of the work of a jurist so eminently qualified was called for.

It is perhaps proper to call attention to the difference in the motives which have impelled the author and the translator to their respective tasks. The former entitles his work a "Contribution to the History of the Roman Law in the Middle Ages," and the purpose of his investigation is to throw light upon the medieval history of the doctrines and dogmas of the *Roman* law. The object, however, with which the translation has been made, is to add to the sources of information concerning the history of the *English* law. Although Dr. Güterbock's work must be regarded as a Roman law production, the nature of its purpose does not prevent its answering equally well the wants of the student of English legal history in sifting such parts of Bracton's learning as are of Roman origin from the more copious materials in his work which are derived from English sources.

In his own notes the translator has cited English and, if need be, French translations of German works as being more generally accessible than the originals. An index and marginal notes have been added to the translation, and the table of contents has been enlarged.

PHILADELPHIA, February, 1866.

PREFACE.

THE English law is remarkable for its originality and for the steady organic consistency of its development. In respect to such legal characteristics the English are indisputably the only modern nation which can be compared to the ancient Romans. In studying the law of these two peoples no one can avoid perceiving parallels and resemblances, which are all the more interesting from the very fact that the Roman law has had no unimportant influence upon the formation of the English. The English law has long been an object of interest and study to the author, and he has chosen for the subject of investigation in these pages that limited period of its contact with the Roman law for which Bracton, the most important of the English medieval law writers, is the great source and authority. He hopes that what is here offered will not be unwelcome as a contribution to the dogmatic history of the Roman law in the middle ages. He would gladly have pursued his investigations to a later period, but has been prevented doing so by the fact that such a task would require a residence in England of some duration.

The author feels the deepest regret that the death of Dr. Biener should have prevented his submitting this work, before publication, to the criticism of one whose knowledge of the English law was so profound, and whose writings have been to him a source alike of suggestion and example.

In conclusion, the author has to express his especial thanks to Dr. Pertz, *Geheime Regierungsrath*, for most obligingly permitting the use of the Berlin library by a non-resident, and to Professor Mittermeyer, *Geheimerath*, for most kindly placing at his disposition valuable works belonging to his private library.

October, 1861.

TABLE OF CONTENTS.

INTRODUCTION.

PART FIRST.

Bracton and His Work—General Investigation.

CHAPTER I.

CHAPTER II.

CHAPTER III.

CHAPTER IV.

CHAPTER V.

Importance of the Roman Law in Bracton.

CHAPTER VI.

Canon Law.

CHAPTER VII.

Bracton's Influence in England—Editions.

PART SECOND.

Detailed Investigation of the Roman Law in Bracton's Work.

CHAPTER VIII.

Introductory.

CHAPTER IX.

Law of Persons.

CHAPTER X.

Law of Things.

Introduction.

CHAPTER XI.

Possession.

CHAPTER XII.

Acquisition of Property—Occupatio, Accessio, Specificatio.

CHAPTER XIII.

Donatio.

CHAPTER XIV.

Usucapio.

CHAPTER XV.

Servitutes.

CHAPTER XVI.

The Law of Inheritance.

CHAPTER XVII.

Dower.

CHAPTER XVIII.

The Law of Obligations.

CHAPTER XIX.

Actions—Procedure—Practice.

CHAPTER XX.

Assisa Novæ Disseisinæ.

CHAPTER XXI.

Criminal Law.

APPENDIX.

BRACTON

AND

HIS RELATION TO THE ROMAN LAW.

INTRODUCTION.

THE influence of the Roman upon the English law has generally been underrated. Our increased familiarity in Germany with the English law has indeed led us to abandon the opinion that it can be regarded as the successful growth of a law purely Germanic in its origin and formation, and that we can find in England that unobstructed development of our Germanic law which has been impeded in our own country. But notwithstanding the abandonment of this error, the equally mistaken view is still prevalent that the development of the English law has been entirely uninfluenced by the Roman, and that it should be considered merely the natural indigenous product of the English soil. This latter opinion was for a long time adopted in England. The Roman law, like everything which came from Rome, was considered by the English as hostile to their national institutions. Certain politically offensive maxims (*e. g.* quod principi placuit, legis habet vigorem) were, indeed, considered special reasons for such an opinion (*a*). English judges and lawyers avoided having anything to do with the Roman law, and were not ashamed to boast of their ignorance of it, and to show aversion and even contempt for it (*b*). So much was the nation imbued with these feelings that we find them expressed even in acts of state (*c*).

German views of the English law.

English views of the Roman law.

(*a*) Fortescue De Laudibus, c. 33, c. 34.

(*b*) See the account of the Abbot of Torum's case (22 Edward III. 1349) in Selden ad Fletam, c. 8, § 5, where Skipwith, an eminent lawyer, declares words referring to the *operis novi nunciatio* to be mere nonsense: "in ceux parolx *contra inhibitionem novi operis* ny ad pas entendement."

(*c*) Thus in 1388 Parliament declared: que ce royalme d'Engleterre n'estait devant ces heures, ne à l'entent du roy nostre dit seignior et seigniors du parlement unque ne serra rulé et governé par la *ley civill.* Rot. Parl., 11 Ric. II.

Such opinions are, however, no longer held in England. A scientific attention has long since been again turned to the Roman law. Judges and legislators have long acknowledged that the Corpus Juris is an authority which is useful, or rather indispensable, for the English law. The investigation of legal history, and especially the closer study of the medieval law books, have produced the conviction that the Roman law, without indeed any formal reception, had at certain times not only been held in esteem, but also had enjoyed a practical authority and a partial validity in England. The same studies have also established the fact that the part of the Roman law in the development and formation of the English had been no inconsiderable one, and one certainly greater than had usually been attributed to it; and that many legal principles and even whole heads of the English law had been derived from the Roman, or had been fundamentally influenced by Roman views. The Roman law can therefore justly be regarded by the English as one of the sources of their Common law. The Civil and the Canon laws have, indeed, always had a special sphere of application over matters which the Common law did not take cognizance of (*d*).

History of the Roman law in England.

The history of the Roman law in England, is still unwritten. Besides its importance for a proper comprehension of the English law, it is of high interest for the history of the Roman law in medieval and modern times. To write it would indeed be no small task. The historian must follow, through the Saxon and first Norman periods, the traces of what was left behind by the Romans; he must study the return of the Roman law with *Vacarius*, and the growth and effect of the new school of Civilians; he must investigate the penetration of the Roman elements into practical usage, and their influence upon the different branches of the English law, just then developing. He must then show how the full development of the national law and the confidence felt in its strength and capacity to

---

(*d*) Matters under the jurisdiction of the Ecclesiastical and Admiralty Courts. *Cf.* Stephen, Commentaries, I. 61–69.

stand alone, produced an antagonism between it and the Roman law, which drove the latter from Westminster Hall; how the Roman law, nevertheless, gained ground in the ecclesiastical courts, and in the Equity system under pretor-chancellors; and finally how, at length, the increase of social and commercial intercourse and the absence of a finished national law of obligations led to the Roman law being appealed to as a Jus Gentium, whose rich materials might supply the deficiencies of the younger law in such matters.

Little has been done towards such a task, and, indeed, even for the collection and preparation of the abundant and varied materials which exist for it. The German works bearing upon the subject include the following: C. F. Wenck's monograph upon Magister Vacarius (1), and the valuable writings of F. A. Biener, comprising pp. 216–230 of his Contributions to the History of Inquisitorial Procedure (2), his article in Mittermeyer's Critical Journal for Foreign Jurisprudence, XIX. 160, upon the "Diffusion of the Roman Law in the Middle Ages, and its Influence upon the English Law" (3), his treatise upon Glanville and Bracton inserted as an appendix in the second edition of Savigny's History of the Roman Law in the Middle Ages, vol. IV. 580–588 (4), and lastly pp. 279 *sq.*, 283 *sq.* of his work on the English Jury (5). Savigny hardly mentions England in his great work: what he says, II. 156–161, bears only upon the Anglo-Saxon period, and, IV. 411–433, upon Vacarius and his contemporaries. Phillips in his Political and Legal History of England, I. 255 *sq.*, 224 *sq.*, has only little of importance (6). The assistance furnished by the English works bearing upon this subject is not less restricted than that derived from the German. Of the older works Selden's

(1) Magister Vacarius primus Juris Romani in Anglia Professor, etc. Leipsic, 1820.—*Tr.*

(2) Beiträge zur Geschichte des Inquisitionsprozesses.—*Tr.*

(3) Kritische Zeitschrift für Rechtswissenschaft des Auslands, XIX. s. 160 ff.: "Die Verbreitung des Röm. Rechts im Mittelalter und der Einfluss desselben auf das Englische Recht."—*Tr.*

(4) Geschichte des Röm. Rechts im Mittelalter.—*Tr.*

(5) Das Englische Geschwornengericht. Leipsic, 1852.—*Tr.*

(6) Englische Reichs- und Rechtsgeschichte.—*Tr.*

Dissertatio ad Fletam (*e*) must be mentioned on account of a sort of sketch of the external history of the Roman law in England, in chapters 3–10, which contains many interesting details, but does not enter into the history of its doctrines and dogmas. Duck's De Usu et Auctoritate Juris Civilis Romanorum in Dominiis Principum Christianorum (*f*), which is almost contemporary with Selden's work, has a considerable portion (pp. 320–409) treating of England, but offers nothing requiring mention. The later English writers upon the history of the law mostly contain only general references to the subject. The best that has been written is still to be found in Reeves's History of the English Law, I. 81 *sq.*, II. 54 *sq.* (*g*). Spence, in his recent work upon the Equitable Jurisdiction of the Court of Chancery, which is of great importance for the history of the English law, has paid much attention to the history of the Roman law in England, and has made researches upon many details of the subject (*h*).

Roman epoch of English legal history.

If the materials for the history of the Roman law in England were brought together, the hundred and fifty years lying between the middle of the twelfth and the end of the thirteenth century would be found to be a most productive period. During that period, while the amalgamation of the various Saxon, Danish, and Norman elements was going on, the legal instincts of the English nation were struggling to develop a uniform domestic law. Marks of the gradual success of this spontaneous effort are seen in the creation of those peculiar legal institutions and characteristics which distinguish the English law from that of other peoples. At this very time the English law was brought into immediate and intimate contact with the Roman law, which was just then one of the principal and most successful objects of the intellectual culture of the middle ages. A new element was thus introduced into the formation of the English law, whose influence

(*e*) Printed with Fleta, 1647 and 1686, and in Hoffmanni Historia Juris Romani; Leipsic, 1737. [Translated by Kelham, London, 1771.—*Tr.*]

(*f*) Lugd. Batav. 1654. [London, 1649, 1653.—*Tr.*]

(*g*) Crabbe's History of the English Law is of much less importance. It is translated into German by Schäffner.

(*h*) See vol. I. 119–121, 123, 131, 235, etc. [See Long's Discourses, 86–92.—*Tr.*]

was so great and the results of which were so important, that the whole of that part of English legal history is very properly styled by Biener its *Roman* epoch. The influence and effects of this new factor are best shown in the law books belonging to that period, the production of which was partially owing to the impulse of the Roman law. The merit of these works is such that they for a long time surpassed the subsequent efforts of English legal literature, and down to the present day they have always been esteemed as important legal authorities. The names of Glanville, Bracton, Fleta, etc. are linked with the adoption and practical use of Roman law in England, just as that of Vacarius is coupled with its introduction. Bracton, however, is in this respect by far the most important, and his great work, "De Legibus et Consuetudinibus Angliæ," occupies the first place among these law books on account of the extent and the value of its contents. It reflects fully and faithfully the then condition of the law, and depicts most clearly both the progress of the Common law, and the influence, operation, and effects of the Roman law.

Bracton.

The subject of the following pages is Bracton, and especially his relation to the Roman law. In them it will be attempted, more fully than has hitherto been done, to determine the general importance of the Roman law in Bracton's work and in Bracton's day, and to make an investigation in detail of the Roman elements in the former which shall separate them from the rest of his legal matter, so that it may be clearly ascertained how far the Roman law was adopted in the different institutions and branches of the English law, and how great was its influence in England at that particular period.

Subject of the present treatise.

PART FIRST.

BRACTON AND HIS WORK.—GENERAL INVESTIGATION.

PART FIRST.

BRACTON AND HIS WORK.—GENERAL INVESTIGATION.

Authors treating of Bracton:

Reeves, History of the English Law, II. 86–90.

Spence, The Equitable Jurisdiction of the Court of Chancery, I. 119 *sq.*, 131, 235.

Biener, Geschichte des Inquisitionsprozesses (History of Inquisitorial Procedure), 220–222.

Von Savigny, Geschichte des Römischen Rechts im Mittelalter (History of the Roman Law in the Middle Ages), Appendix XXIV (*Biener*), 583 *sq.*

Biener, Das Englische Geschwornengericht (The English Jury), II. 286. (1)

CHAPTER I.

BRACTON'S LIFE—DATE OF HIS WORK.

Henricus de Bracton flourished in the middle of the thirteenth century. The usual as well as the correct spelling of his name is Bracton (*a*). The bio-

Biographical details.

(*a*) The name of Bracton was not uncommon at that period. In the Placitorum Abbreviatio there are mentioned Thomas, Robert, and Humfred de Bracton on f. 11, and a de Bracton f. 19. The name occurs in two passages of the work itself, f. 1, ego *Henricus de Bracton* animum erexi, and f. 188 b. in the discussion of error in nomine:—ut si quis alium nominat Henricum de Brocheton, ubi nominari deberet *Henricum de Bracton;* item......nominando Henricum

(1) To these should be added the chapter on Bracton in Long's Discourses, pp. 93–108, and the biographical notice of Bracton in Foss's Judges of England, II. 249.—*Tr.*

graphical details which have come down to us concerning Bracton are very meagre; even the years of his birth and death are unknown. That he was a professional lawyer is shown by his book, which could only have been written by one familiar with the actual details of the practice of the law. We need therefore have no hesitation in identifying him with the Justiciarius Bracton, mentioned in judicial records of 1246, 1252, 1255, and other years (*b*). In the notice of Bracton in Pauli's History of England, it is said that he was a clerk (*c*). This may have been the case, and would indeed account for certain theological remarks found occasionally in his book (*d*). His work shows that he was most familiar with the Roman law, and that he had enjoyed an unusually excellent education therein, but Spence's assertion that he taught the Roman law at Oxford in the middle

---

de Brachton ubi nominari deberet *Henricum de Bracton.* The spelling *Bracton* has not, however, been always followed. Selden ad Fletam, c. 2, § 2, has given others: Breton, Bratton, Brecton, Britton, Bryckton. [Bratton is a modern local name in England. The name was originally Brachton and Bracton, but was transformed to Bratton by the omission of the guttural, in accordance with a well-known linguistic law.—*Tr.*]

(*b*) Placitorum Abbreviatio, f. 138, ex 36 Henry III. (1252): "Nisi *Henricus de Bratton* prius venerit in partes Devoniæ;" ibid. "et lectum est breve Dno. *H. de Bratton* directum, per quod Dom. Rex ipsum Justiciarium," etc. In the New Fœdera, I. 320, there is a record of an assise of the 39 Henry III. (1255), held "coram justiciariis H. de Bathonia, *Henrico de Bracton,*" etc. Spence, I. 119 m., gives a final concord made 30 Henry III. (1246), "coram H. de Bathonia, Jeremia de Caxton et *Henrico de Bracton,* justiciariis et aliis domini regis fidelibus." [In the Excerpta Rot. Fin. there are many records of payments for assises before Bracton from the years 1250 to 1267, inclusive; see the index under *Bratton.* From these entries and those in Dugd. Chron. 13, Abbrev. Plac. 128 (three times), Seld. Heng., 120, Bracton was probably upon the judicial bench without interruption during the whole period from 1245 to 1267, if not longer. In 38 Henry III. (A.D. 1254), he received a grant by patent, for his chambers, of the London mansion of the deceased Earl of Derby during the minority of the son and heir of the Earl. (Dugd. Orig., 56.)—*Tr.*]

(*c*) Pauli, Gesch. von England, III. 823. [Bracton was Archdeacon of Barnstaple; v. Foss, l. c.—*Tr.*]

(*d*) E.g. f. 2, the denunciation of judicial immorality with quotations from St. Augustine; f. 106, quotations from the Book of Job, c. 39; from Deuteronomy, c. 86. Bracton, f. 188 b. (v. note (*a*) above), adds to his own name by way of example the qualifications precentor and dean, perhaps referring to his former station.

of the thirteenth century has not been conclusively established (*e*).

The legal treatise of which Bracton is the author, and which has alone rescued his name from oblivion, bears the following title in the printed editions:

Bracton's work.

Henrici de Bracton de Legibus et Consuetudinibus Angliæ Libri quinque, in varios tractatus distincti.

It is first of all indispensable in this investigation, to ascertain the time when the work was composed. It is certain that it was written in the reign of Henry III., for the phrases *Rex noster*, *rex H.*, *qui nunc est* and the like, show that king to have been still living. It is true that there is *one* passage which alludes to Edward I. and to a change in the law made by the statute of Westminster of 1275, but it is of no significance or importance (*f*). The whole contents of the work as well as other decisive considerations, prove that it must be discarded as the subsequent interpolation of a foreign hand. Such indeed the passage would seem to be from its external appearance, as it is

Investigation of its date.

(*e*) Spence, I. 119 m., cites as authority the anonymous author of the article on Bracton in the Penny Cyclopædia. The authority for this must be Duck, De Usu et Auctoritate Juris Civilis, 382; who says: "erat enim Bractonus *juris cæsarei professor Oxonii.*" Thornton, the author of an epitome of Bracton, styles his work, Summa......composita a magistro H. de Bryctona. Does the term magister refer to any academic functions? [In the church of St. Michael at Minehead, in Somersetshire, there is a monument with a robed effigy and a tomb supposed to be Bracton's. Near Minehead is Bratton Court, where our author is said to have lived, and his family resided for many generations. This is not, however, the only place of that name in England which claims him; see Murray's Handbook for Somersetshire, p. 203. References to pedigrees of Bratton and Bracton are given in Sims's Index to Pedigrees in the British Museum.—*Tr.*]

(*f*) This passage is on f. 253 b. in the body of the *breve de assisa mortis antecessoris:*

> et si obiit post ultimum reditum regis Johannis patris nostri de Hibernia in Angliam (*et tempore regis Eduardi mutatus* fuit terminus iste post coronationem regis *Henrici patris ipsius regis Eduardi*).

This new limitation was in fact introduced by the statute 3 Edward I. c. 39. The addition is therefore made after that statute, probably by the hand of a practitioner.

found placed between brackets. As to a more precise determination of the time of the composition of Bracton's work, opinions differ. The English authorities consider it to have been written between the years 1262 and 1268 (Spence *circa* 1270). Biener, however, thinks that Bracton composed his work within the years 1240–1255 (*g*). I cannot myself accept either of these views. After examining and comparing the data, I am of opinion that the work was written within the years 1256–1259.

The great number of judicial cases, the dates of which are given in the respective years of the king's reign, and the relation which the work bears to particular statutes and to different events of the time, serve as bases for the determination of this question.

Bracton's work must at all events be more recent than the year 1236, even to suppose the earliest possible date, for the statute of Merton, promulgated in that year (20 Henry III.), is expressly mentioned in two places, and some of its provisions are given (*h*). However, not only the year 1236 but also the year 1240, the commencement of the period maintained by Biener, are both too early. For it is not the fact, as Biener thinks, that Bracton cites no cases dated later than 22–24 Henry III. (1238–40), as I have found a considerable number belonging to later years, viz. 30–33 and even 38 Henry III. (1246–1254) (*i*). The time when Bracton's work was written is thus made far later than 1240, and even as late as 1255, the end of the period maintained by Biener. Another decisive circumstance, however, which has hitherto remained unobserved, compels us to place still later our earliest limit. Bracton gives the following example, f. 47, in speaking of conditional *donationes:*

> "ut si dicatur: do tibi tantum terræ......*si Comes Ricardus effectus fuerit Rex Alemannus.*"

(*g*) Reeves, II. 90. Spence, 120 b. Biener, Inq. Pr., 220. Eng. Geschw., II. 28 b.

(*h*) Bracton, 227, 416 b.

(*i*) E.g. Bracton, 413: anno regni regis Henrici tricesimo; f. 414: anno tricesimo primo; f. 241: anno regis H. XXXII; f. 339 b.: anno regis H. XXXVIII.

Bracton must here have alluded to the election of *Richard Earl of Cornwall*, brother of Henry III., as German Emperor. It is hardly credible that he should have accidentally thought of the possibility of such an event, and we cannot but believe that he knew of it as having already taken place or as nearly impending. The chronology of that election and of its attendant circumstances is well known: William of Holland died in January, 1256, the first proposals to Richard were in the spring following, and the negotiations with the princes of the Empire were made during the further course of the year. Richard's election took place on January 13th, 1257, and his coronation in the following May (*j*). These facts most certainly demonstrate that Bracton had not completely finished his work *before the years* 1256 or 1257, and that it is impossible that Biener's dates can be correct. Whether we must descend even later than the time thus ascertained will depend upon the meaning of another passage, f. 159, which quotes a case of the 46th year of Henry III. (1262) (*k*). If this citation be genuine and accurate, we must of course assent to the English view that Bracton's work is more recent than 1262. Such, however, is not the fact. It must be remarked in the first place that this case is the sole citation from a series of years, which being the most recent should have furnished most material to the author. The possibility of an error in the date of the case is also increased by the discordance of the texts, one of which has the manifestly false reading 56 instead of 46 (*l*), while an emendation of 36 reconciles it with our other conclusions. It must be here recollected that XXXXVI, and not XLVI, was written in the manuscripts. Against the genuineness of the passage is the fact that it is not interwoven in the text according to Bracton's usage, but stands alone without any connection with what goes before, very much as if it were the marginal note of another and later hand. The conjecture that it is

(*j*) For details v. Pauli, Gesch. von England, III. 707–710.

(*k*) Casus de *Petro de Sabaudia*......coram consilio dom. regis apud Westmon. ......anno regni regis H. XLVI. de termino Paschæ.

(*l*) 56 Henry III. = 1272; Petrus de Sabaudia, however, was dead in 1269; New Fœdera, I. 482.

either an error or (as Biener thinks) a subsequent addition, becomes a certainty, if we consider the internal evidence, for it can be proved that Bracton must have written his work before 1262. The English authorities indeed fix upon 1267 as the latest possible date, on the ground that Bracton could not have avoided mentioning the important changes in the law made by the *statute of Marlbridge* (November, 1267, 52 Henry III.), had its provisions been known to him. In point of fact he could not have known of another statute, made some eight years earlier in 1259 (43 Henry III.), entitled "*Provisiones factæ per Regem et Consilium suum.*" This statute of 1259, which appears to have been made under the influence of the council which had been forced upon the king by the barons (2), made alterations in the law which were repeated in certain provisions of the statute of Marlbridge (*m*). Not only does Bracton pass over in entire silence the important provisions of the statute of 1259 concerning feudal tenures and the actions relating to dower and advowsons, but he also expounds the old law and dwells upon its defects (*n*). It must therefore be concluded that this statute could not have been known to him when he was writing his work, and that

(*m*) Printed in the Statutes of the Realm, I. 8. The preamble runs: Anno ab incarnatione Dn. MCCL⁰ nono regni autem H. regis fil. regis Johann. XLIII⁰ convenientibus apud Westmonast. in quindena Sti. Michaelis ipso domino rege et magnatibus suis, de communi consilio et consensu dictorum regis et Magnatum factæ sunt provisiones subscriptæ, etc.

(*n*) Bracton, 247.

(2) By the provisions of Oxford, which had been forced upon the king in 1258, his power was, in a great measure, superseded. While they were enforced, the judges depended for their continuance in office upon the authority of those who had imposed them upon the king. During this period the provisions, or statute of 1259 mentioned in the text, were enacted at Westminster (43 H. 3, Stat. R., fol 8). Bracton—as printed records prove—in the mean time, and afterwards, exercised his judicial functions without interruption (see particularly Rot. Claus., 44 H. 3, cited Dugd. Chron. 19, also Rot. Fin. II., A.D. 1258 to 1267). Political reasons therefore would not have prevented him from referring to the enactments of 1259 if they had been passed before he wrote. Indeed it may be doubted whether the binding effect of these provisions of 1259 (as distinguished from those of 1258) was ever disputed by anybody. Before the re-enactment at Marlbridge in 1267 (52 H. 3) the provisions of 1259 (43 H. 3) had been published in 1260 (44 H. 3) and in 1262 (47 H. 3), as appears

the completion of his book must have been before the year 1259, and consequently before the date of the case in question (1262). Under these circumstances that date ceases to be of any importance.

In the foregoing remarks we have sought to show that it is nearly certain that Bracton's work was composed within the years 1256–1259, and conjecture may go yet a step further. As our author speaks of the election of Richard as a contingent event, it can scarcely be supposed that, after it was known to have actually taken place, he would have made its occurrence the subject of a condition. Bracton too, in another place, calls Richard, *Comes Ricardus* (*o*), while after his election he is spoken of by his contemporaries and in official documents under titles expressing his new rank, such as *Rex Alemannorum*, *Rex Romanorum*, and *Rex Ricardus* (*p*).

(*o*) Bracton, 288 b.: ut si interrogat, quis fuit apud concilium London., et respondeat quis, quod Rex et *Comes Ricardus* (ut credit). [This must have been the Parliament or assembly of magnates at London after Easter, A.D. 1254 (38 H. III.), mentioned by M. Paris (Edit. 1640), 887. The king's message was sent to them under his seal, and they waited in vain for three weeks the arrival of Earl Richard.—*Tr.*]

(*p*) E.g. Mathew Paris (Edit. 1640), 160, 161 *sq.*; New Fœdera, I. 353, where he is first called "Ricardus......Romanorum in regem electus;" ibid. 356, 358, 377, 396.

from the close roll of the former, and patent roll of the latter year cited Stat. Realm, fol. 8; and there is an entry before justices itinerant A.D. 1261 (45 H. 3), quia *de novo provisum est per consilium domini Regis* quod murdrum de cætero non adjudicetur in regno ubi infortunium tantummodo præsentatur, sed locum teneat de interfectis per feloniam et non aliter (Fleta, Edit. in fol. f. 70, note) in a case in which one of the provisions of 1259 was acted upon as in force. It is the one which was re-enacted by the 25th chapter of the statute of Marlbridge. No such enactment could have been in force when Bracton, 135, wrote, de iis qui mortui sunt per infortunium, nullum erit murdrum, *licet in quibusdam partibus de consuetudine aliter observetur.* Of such local usage, contrary to the general usage as he states it, an instance in 32 H. 3, Gloucestershire, may be cited from the same note to Fleta. After the statute of 1259 no such usage could have been observable anywhere within the realm.

It is perhaps not here out of place to refer to the record printed in Madox, Exch. (4to.), II. 257 b., from which it appears that in the year 1258 (42 H. 3) Bracton was called on to return to the proper depository the rolls of an iter of the early part of the reign of Henry III., to which he had made frequent references in his text, and which, doubtless, had been in his possession while writing the work.—*Tr.*

The conclusion, therefore, does not seem hazardous that it was before the actual election and pending the previous negotiation, *i.e.* in the course of the year 1256, that Bracton wrote at least that part of his work in which such a contingency as Earl Richard's election would naturally suggest itself to him (3).

ADDITIONAL NOTE TO CHAPTER I.

Date of Bracton's work.

Bracton was probably engaged for many years in writing his book; and he may, after his work of authorship had ceased, have made occasional additions to the manuscript without revising the original text. Biener may have found one or more passages written as early as 1240. The passage on fol. 327 b., cited post Chapter XVI., note (*r*), was probably written before the death of Eleanor of Brittany in 1241. The phrase quamdiu casus regis duraverit probably meant *as long as she might live.* She was, on account of this *casus regis*, a prisoner of state until her death. In the passage on fol. 115 b., *proponi solent verba ista per Martinum de Pateshull,* the word *solent* in the present tense, might be supposed to import that Martin de Pateshull, who died in 1229 (M. Paris, Ed. 1640, p. 363), was living when it was written. But the text, if corrupt or loosely written, may mean that judges were, in Bracton's time, in the habit of using the words which had first been used by M. de Pateshull.

It has been clearly shown in the text that Bracton's work of authorship continued until 1256 or 1257. He was, however, on the judicial bench as late as July, 1267. The reference, f. 159, to the case in 46 H. III. (A.D. 1262), may therefore have been added by himself. But that he made no general revision of his work after 1259 seems to be sufficiently established by his omissions to correct his text by references to the statute of that year.

---

(3) The words of Bracton cited above are si Comes Ricardus *effectus* fuerit Rex Alemannus (not *electus* fuerit). After Richard's election, which became known in England in January, 1257, it was for some time uncertain whether he would ever be crowned—*effectus* Rex. His coronation in May, 1257, was forcibly opposed in the interval with bloodshed. The passage in Bracton may therefore have been written between January, 1257, and the time when the coronation of May, 1257, became known in England.—*Tr.*

The consideration of Bracton's doctrine concerning the king's being suable is not without interest in this connection. From Bracton's remarks, 171 b., 212, it appears that redress from the king was not obtainable by suit or action against him, but only by way of petition. From what is said, 382 b., it appears that where the king was a warrantor he could not be vouched to warrant, for non potest vocari sicut vocantur privatæ personæ quia summoneri non potest per breve. His remarks on 171 b. are, however, qualified by the following striking passage: *nisi sit qui dicat quod universitas regni et baronagium suum hoc facere debeat et possit in curia ipsius regis.* This passage Bracton may have written long after he wrote others concerning royal power in England, which on 5 b., 34, 107, he labors to distinguish from Roman imperial power, but without clearly doing so.

The passage just given from 171 b. was probably written between the parliaments of 1255 and 1258. The parliament of 1255 exacted from the king certain concessions which he peremptorily refused (M. Paris, 904, 905). At the parliament of Oxford, in 1258, he was compelled to make these and other concessions. By these provisions of Oxford, he was subjected, as his father had been in 1215, to the control of a standing executive council (Rymer, I. 654, 655 and additions New Fœdera, I. 377, 378; Chron. Lond., 37; M. Par. Addit. 215, etc.). The result of his endeavors to shake off this control was the civil war which began six years afterwards, and ended in the reestablishment of his former authority. It is interesting historically that this passage of Bracton as to the possibility of a compulsory limitation of the royal authority, was probably written while the revolutionary measures attempted at Oxford in 1258 were in prospect or agitation.

English antiquarians have thought that Bracton's doctrine that the king is not suable, was contradicted as to the age of Bracton by the year books (22 E. III. 3 b., 24 E. III. 55 b., and 43 E. III. 22), which state that in the time of Henry III., and previously, the king could be sued as any other person, though it had afterwards been ordained otherwise by Edward I. One of the judges remarked that he had himself seen an original process against King Henry. But records of the reign of John show that before Magna Charta he could not be sued, or could prevent the trial of a suit against himself (Rot. Cur. Reg. Mich., 1 Joh., print. vol. II. pp. 77, 78, 95). Records of John's reign, however, show also that while that king was in subjection to the executive council established by his Magna Charta, he was sued in several instances by those whom he had, in the previous troubles, dispossessed extrajudicially of their land (Close Roll, 17 Joh., print. vol. I. p. 216). The statement of the judge therefore who had seen such process against Henry III. may be fully credited if it is considered as applicable to the period in and for some time after 1258, when the provisions of Oxford were acted upon as in force. But the great charters of his reign (A.D. 1216, 1217, 1225) contained no provision subjecting him to the control of a standing executive council such as had been forced upon his father, or such as was forced upon himself in 1258. Bracton, therefore, *writing before that year*, was doubtless right in his doctrine that the king was not suable adversarily. In the pacification carried into effect by the statutory edict of Kenilworth (51 H. 3, A.D. 1266, 1267), it was provided that every one should sue for justice to the King's Court, and should answer in justice, as had been hitherto usual before the time of the late troubles (Stat. Realm, I. fol. 12). Whether this enactment applies to the question is perhaps doubtful. But from records of the year 1272 (56 H. 3, Rot. Fin., vol. II. pp. 508, 514, 515, 563, 564, 574), it appears that when lands of a deceased tenant in capite were taken into the king's hands the only remedy of his widow for her dower, of his coheiresses for partition, or of an heir entitled to restitution in order to obtain it, was by petition, and that redress was accorded as of grace and not as of right. Before this, while the king was the prisoner of De Montfort, who conducted the government in the king's name, the form of proceeding in such cases seems to have also been by petition (9 Nov. 1264, 49 H. III. ib. pp. 416, 417).

Of the troubles of that reign one of the causes appears from the chronicles to have been, that justice was not compulsorily obtainable from great officers of state, or from members of the royal family. That it could not in fact have been obtainable compulsorily from the king seems therefore clear.—*Translator.*

CHAPTER II.

CHARACTER OF BRACTON'S WORK—SYSTEM—METHOD.

THE character of Bracton's work is placed in a very clear light, if we compare it with the legal treatise known as Glanville's, which was written some seventy years earlier.

Glanville and Bracton.

Ranulph de Glanville was the well-known Great Justiciary and general of Henry II. He is usually regarded as the author of the treatise, which has come down to us with the following title:

Glanville's work.

> *Tractatus de legibus et consuetudinibus regni Angliæ* tempore regis Henrici secundi compositus, justitiæ gubernacula tenente illustro viro Ranulpho de Glanvilla.

The date of Glanville's work is shortly anterior to the year 1190 (*a*). The title, like Bracton's, is: De Legibus et Consuetudinibus Angliæ; a phraseology which seems to indicate it to be a view of the whole Anglo-Norman law. The author, however, confesses in his preface that it was out of the power of any one in that age to embody the whole law and customs of the land in the shape of a general view in writing. From the outset he confines himself to matters relating to the

(*a*) Concerning Glanville, v. Reeves I. 221–227. Phillips, Englische Rechtsgeschichte I. 231–242; Biener, Inq. Pr. 218–220 and in Savigny IV. 580–583; Spence I. 119. Besides the editions mentioned by Biener, there is one in the Kœnigsberg library printed in London by Richard Tottel without date. I cannot decide whether or not, it is the same as Sir William Staunford's edition of 1554. It is well known that Glanville's authorship is disputed, but there are preponderating reasons in favor of it, especially in the mention made of him in different forms given as examples. [See also Beames's introductory remarks to his translation of Glanville, and Foss, Judges of England, I. 376.—*Tr.*]

practice of the Curia Regis and to the principles of law most frequently arising in that court (*b*). We must not therefore expect to find a *system of law* in Glanville. Such an attempt, as the author himself says, must have failed, in consequence of the then confused state of the law, which was still in the first commencement of its progress toward being harmoniously perfected and consolidated. What Glanville gives, is a short sketch of the course and forms of procedure intended for immediate practical use (ad adjuvandam memoriam). He only subordinately develops and explains the substantive rules of right; these are, for the most part, only discussed incidentally, and chiefly in their relation to and bearing upon legal procedure, to the rules of which they are generally appended. These circumstances have given rise to that poverty upon many matters of which the reader is often painfully conscious, and to the often superficial and interrupted commentary connected therewith, which is especially obvious in the later books (*c*).

Character of Bracton's work.

It is quite otherwise with Bracton. The development of the English law had been great and constant during the seventy years lying between him and Glanville. The completion of the feudal system, the new forms of action (assises), the recognition of judicial decisions as new authorities and productive sources of law, the impulse given by the Roman law, and finally the scholastic spirit animating the lawyers, had since Glanville's time developed the English law into an artistically organized and often overrefined system. The difficulty of mastering the subject was therefore constantly increasing, and a knowledge of the law was no longer to be acquired by its mere use, but only by a regular course of study. The law had now reached a stage

---

(*b*) Glanville; prologus: Leges autem et jura regni scripto universaliter concludi nostris temporibus omnino quidem impossibile est cum propter scribentium ignorantiam, cum propter *earum multitudinem confusam;* verum sunt quædam in Curia generalia et frequentius usitata quæ scripto commendare non mihi videtur præsumtuosum.

(*c*) Biener's conjecture, that Glanville died before the entire completion of his work, is not improbable. His death occurred in 1190 at the siege of Acre.

in which a legal science is naturally wont to be developed. This new scientific tendency, the obvious insufficiency of a jus non scriptum (*d*), together with the multitude of new questions, doubts, and deficiencies, explain the want of some written view of the rules of the law. Such a work was needed not only to direct the studies now necessary and to guide practitioners themselves, but also to protect suitors against ignorant or malevolent judges, who at that period might very possibly make their own arbitrary will a substitute for law.

It is Bracton's merit to have perceived this want and to have taken upon himself the task of supplying it. His work, which is the first scientific commentary upon English law, at the same time pursues the practical purposes just referred to. He remarks in his preface:

> "Cum autum hujusmodi leges et consuetudines per insipientes et minus doctos,......sæpius trahantur ad abusum, et quæ stant in dubiis, et opinionibus multotiens pervertuntur a majoribus, qui *potius proprio arbitrio quam legum auctoritate casus decidant*......ad instructionem saltem minorum animum erexi ad vetera judicia justorum perscrutanda......*facta ipsorum consilia et responsa......in unam summam redigendo*" (*e*).

The contents of the work correspond to these aims. The author displays to the reader a clear picture of the then existing law, drawn in copious detail and not in general outlines. His view of the law is strictly faithful to truth, and is digested into a completely logical system. In it, all parts of the law receive consideration: procedure in its manifold complexities, its minute formalities, and all its stages; the substantive rules of law and property, which are no longer made subordinate to those of procedure; the feudal system and its legal constitution; the different interests in immovables; the law of movables; and finally, that of obligations, which is, however, but briefly considered. Besides these,

---

(*d*) "Sola Anglia usa est in finibus suis jure non scripto;" Bracton, f. 1.

(*e*) *Cf.* Bracton, 1 b.: Intentio autem est......instruere et docere omnes, qui edoceri desiderant, qualiter—etc.

criminal law and procedure are treated with equal detail, and even questions of political and ecclesiastical law are included within the range of the commentary. Strictly speaking, the commentary is limited to the general common law of the realm, but there are also occasional reflections upon particular provincial customs as hints for the judges on their eyres (*f*). The relation of Glanville's to Bracton's work is therefore very much that of a collection of legal forms to an elaborate and systematic treatise upon the law.

Its style. In the matter of style also, Bracton is far above his predecessor. Both use the Latin, the literary and judicial language of the times in which they lived (*g*). But while Glanville adheres intentionally to the often barbarous judicial style of his day—"stylo vulgari et verbis curialibus utens" (Prol.)—Bracton writes a very readable Latin. Although far from being classical, it always is adapted to the subject, and expresses the author's meaning clearly and suitably, while sometimes rising to a certain higher strain. Bracton's style need in no case avoid a comparison with that of his contemporaries, the Italian law writers especially (*h*). Here and there the monotony of the commentary is broken by the introduction of versus memoriales (*i*), or by digressions, which show the general cultivation of the author (*j*).

Its division. The work in the printed editions is divided into five books (*k*). The two first books are entitled *de rerum divisione* and *de adquirendo rerum dominio*,

---

(*f*) Bracton, 12, 330. Consuetudo in civitate Lincolniæ, in villa de Gipevico.

(*g*) Anglo-Saxon law phrases are occasionally found in Bracton; see f. 40. 124 b. 150 b. 154 b. 185.

(*h*) Reeves, II. 88, goes quite too far when he makes Bracton's style superior to that of most of his contemporaries.

(*i*) E.g. f. 18 b.: Scito, quod *ut* modus est, *si* conditio, *quia* causa. F. 217 b.: Cum sit modus in rebus, sunt certi denique fines. F. 16 b.: Re, verbis, scripto, consensu, traditione, junctura, vestes sumere pacta solent. F. 438.: Nam dicunt *E* vel *A* quotquot nascuntur ab Eva.

(*j*) E.g. The astronomical explanation of the intercalary day, f. 359.

(*k*) Selden ad Fletam, 2, § 4, remarks that this division is not in all the manuscripts. It may not indeed have originated with Bracton.

and are divided into chapters and paragraphs. The other books have no headings, and are divided first into tracts, and these again into chapters and paragraphs. The third book contains two tracts, entitled respectively, *de actionibus* and *de corona*. The fourth book is composed of seven tracts, the first five of which are called after the assises of which they treat; the two last tracts are entitled respectively *de actione dotis* and *de ingressu*. The fifth book contains five tracts, entitled respectively *de breve de recto*, *de essoniis*, *defaltis*, *warrantia*, and *de exceptionibus*. Bracton is quoted in two ways, either according to the paging, or according to the division just mentioned (e.g. IV. 1. 20. § 4., i.e. Lib. IV. tract. 1. c. 20. § 4). Many prefer the former method on account of the great length of many paragraphs and the agreement of the paging in the two editions, and I have myself adopted it.

Bracton's system does not entirely coincide with the division just spoken of. The matter of the work is divided into two principal, although unequal, parts. The first part, concluding with Lib. III. tract. 1. c. 4. fol. 104 a., contains the substantive and fundamental rules of the law; the other, running from fol. 104 b. to the end, is devoted to legal procedure. This division, however, is not rigorously adhered to in details. The main features of the system of law upon which the first part is based are not original with Bracton, but are taken from the well-known trichotomy of Justinian's Institutes, "quod omne jus pertinet vel ad personas, vel ad res, vel ad actiones." Its analysis is as follows (¹):

Bracton's system.

The Introduction, Lib. I. c. 1–5. f. 1–4, after which are treated:

Analysis thereof.

A. *De personis* et de divisione personarum (*l*), Lib. I. c. 6–11. f. 4 b.–7 b.

(*l*) The heading of the first book, "de rerum divisione," in the printed editions, is manifestly incorrect.

(¹) *Cf.* the analysis or summary of Bracton in Reeves, II. 86.—*Tr.*

B. *De rebus.*

- I. *De rerum divisione* Lib. I. c. 12. f. 7 b.–8.
- II. *De adquirendo rerum dominio:*
  - AA. *Ex jure naturali:* herein of occupatio, accessio, specificatio, Lib. II. c. 1–3. f. 8 b.–10 b.
  - BB. *Ex jure civili:*
    1. Ex causa *donationis* inter vivos (*m*) Lib. II. c. 5–25. f. 11–59 b.
       - a. rerum corporalium Lib. II. c. 5–22. f. 11 to 53.
         Under this rubric:
         de possessione, traditione, Lib. II. c. 17 to 21. f. 38 b.–52;
         de usucaptione, Lib. II. c. 22. f. 51 b.–52 b.;
       - b. rerum incorporalium Lib. II. c. 23–25. f. 52 b.–60.
    2. Ex causa donationis mortis causa Lib. II. c. 26. f. 60–61.
    3. Ex causa emptionis Lib. II. c. 27. f. 61 b.
    4. De locato, conducto Lib. II. c. 28. f. 62.
    5. Ex causa successionis (*n*) Lib. II. c. 29–38. f. 62–91 b.
    6. Ex causa dotis Lib. II. c. 39. 40. f. 92–98.

C. *De actionibus* Lib. III. tract. 1. c. 1–4. f. 98 b.–104 b.
Under this; *de obligationibus* ibid. c. 2. f. 99–101.

The transition from the first to the second part of Bracton's system is brought about by the commentary upon courts and jurisdictions, connected with the division of actions. The discussion of that subject occupies chapters 5–12 of the first tract, and the first two chapters of the second tract of the third book. The commentary upon procedure then begins on f. 118, and treats first of criminal matters. Its analysis is as follows:

(*m*) The donatio inter vivos in the English law comprehended all manner of alienations of a feudal character, and is not to be likened to the Roman donation. *Cf.* infra, Chapter XIII.

(*n*) Under this head Bracton treats of wardship and the legal relations derived from tenure (homagium, relevium etc.).

A. *Actiones criminales:*

I. Crimina capitalia Lib. III. tr. 2. c. 3–35. f. 118 to 154.

Under this: de crimine læsæ majestatis Lib. III. tr. 2. c. 3. f. 118–120.

de crimine homicidii Lib. III. tr. 2. c. 4–22. f. 120 b.–143 b.

de furto (*o*) Lib. III. tr. 2. c. 32–35. f. 150 b.–154 b.

II. Crimina minora Lib. III. tr. 2. c. 36. 37. f. 155 to 159 b.

B. *Actiones civiles:*

AA. *Actiones reales.*

I. *Possessoriæ:*

(A). de possessione propria:

1. liberi tenementi,—*assisa novæ disseisinæ* Lib. IV. tr. 1. c. 2–36. f. 160–220;
2. servitutum et jurium — *assisa de communia* vel de nocumento Lib. IV. tr. 1. c. 37–50. f. 221–236 b.;
3. juris patronatus—*assisa ultimæ præsentationis* Lib. IV. tr. 2. f. 237–252;

(B). de possessione aliena:

1. *Assisa mortis antecessoris,* Lib. IV. tr. 3. f. 252–280 b.
2. Breve *de consanguinitate,* Lib. IV. tr. 4. f. 281–285.
3. *Assisa utrum* (*p*), Lib. IV. tr. 5. f. 285 b.–296.
4. *Actio dotis,* Lib. IV. tr. 6. f. 296–317 b.

II. *Petitoriæ,* vel de causa proprietatis:

1. Breve de *ingressu* Lib. IV. tr. 7. f. 318 to 327 b.

(*o*) In chapters XXVI.–XXXVII., some other crimes are treated of, viz., de plagis, roberia, combustione, raptu virginum etc.

(*p*) The assisa novæ disseisinæ corresponds to the remedium spoliationis of the then Canon law. The assisa ultimæ præsentationis was the possessory action for advowsons. The assisa mortis antecessoris enabled heirs to recover a seisin of realty resembling the bonorum possessio of the Roman law, and the breve de consanguinitate served similar purposes. The assisa utrum was for the purpose of deciding, an feudum sit laicum vel ecclesiasticum. All assises applied only to immovables.

2. Breve de *recto* Lib. V. f. 327 b.–436.
Under this (²);
a. de summonitione et essoniis Lib. V. tr. 1 and 2. f. 333–364;
b. de defaltis Lib. V. tr. 3. f. 364 b.–380;
c. de warrantia Lib. V. tr. 4. f. 380 b.–399 (*q*).
d. de exceptionibus Lib. V. tr. 5. c. 1–30. f. 399 b.–439.

BB. *De actione personali* Lib. V. tr. 5. c. 31. 32. f. 439–443 b.

CC. *De actione mixta* Lib. V. tr. 5. c. 33. f. 443. 444.

So much for Bracton's system.—His method of treatment in details, presents nothing which requires special examination. The effect of the education which Bracton undoubtedly received in the contemporary school of Roman jurisprudence, is plainly seen in the general character of his commentary. Thus, like Placentin, Azo and other Glossators of the age, he arranges his subject by distributing its divisions under interrogatory headings, such as: "quid sit donatio? qualiter dividatur? quis donare possit, quis non? quæ res possit donari et quæ non? cui donare possit et cui non? quæ exiguntur ad hoc, quod valeat donatio?" etc. (*r*). There is this difference, however, between Bracton and the Glossators: with the latter, the exegetical character of the commentary is prominent, while with Bracton it naturally gives way to the dogmatic, and especially the practical, con-

Bracton's method.

(*q*) The breve de ingressu was used for recovering the possession of immovables in cases where it had originally been voluntarily parted with. The breve de recto was, to speak in Roman law language, a vindication for land [*cf.* Spence, I. 219.—*Tr.*]. Essoniæ were the grounds excusing those who would otherwise be in contumacy (defalta). Warrantia was the engagement to secure against eviction.

(*r*) Bracton, 11 *et al.*

(²) Reeves, II. 87, analyzes the fifth book somewhat differently. In the table of contents it is entitled Liber quintus de recto, but in the heading on f. 327 b. it is described as Liber quintus, qui dividitur in quinque tractatus, quorum primus est de recto.—*Tr.*

sideration of the law. The practical point of view is much the most important with our author.

Finally, when we consider the clearness and simplicity of Bracton's commentary, the richness of his matter, examples and forms, together with his apt and appropriate handling of doubtful points and questions, we cannot fail to assign his book a high rank among works of its kind, and acknowledge that it completely fulfills the author's intended purposes.

His merit.

CHAPTER III.

BRACTON'S SOURCES AND AUTHORITIES—THOSE OF ENGLISH ORIGIN.

Domestic sources.

THE sources from which Bracton derives the rich materials, which he has made use of in his work, are partly of domestic and partly of foreign origin. We shall begin with the first. Bracton styles the English law a *jus non scriptum, consuetudinarium:*

> "Cum autem in fere omnibus regionibus utantur legibus et jure scripto, *sola Anglia* usa est in suis finibus jure non scripto et consuetudine" (*a*).

Those in writing.

There was in fact but a small portion of the law which was then handed down in written sources. These latter included only some few statutes (*b*), Glanville's treatise, and some private compilations of old laws, partly obsolete and partly spurious, which went under the names of former kings (Edward the Confessor, William the Conqueror, etc.) (*c*). The degree of culture, however, at which the English law had arrived, was such that a new and copious source of development had been opened. The

(*a*) Bracton, f. 1.

(*b*) Except the different charters of liberties (Magna Charta etc.) and their confirmations, these were only, strictly speaking, *the Statute of Merton* and the so-called *statutum de anno bissextile*, the former 20 Henry III., and the latter 40 (according to some 21) Henry III.

(*c*) Upon the laws of Edward the Confessor and those called William the Conqueror's and Henry the First's, v. Phillips, Engl. Rechtsgeschichte I. 184–222. It is worthy of remark that Bracton seems to refer to the first of these in a passage, f. 124 b.: Et *secundum legis Eduardi regis*, omnis qui est aetatis duodecim annorum facere debet sacramentum in visu franci plegio etc. [See also Thorpe's Ancient Laws, preface and pp. 190, 191, 215.—*Tr.*]

knowledge of the law, at least in its details, instead of remaining the common property of the nation, was gradually becoming a monopoly of those engaged in its practice. The law was now best ascertained from the knowledge residing in the breast of the judges. Their judicial decisions were now the best evidence of the validity of legal principles, became legal rules for future observance, and were the means of developing and improving the law. Attention had therefore already been turned to the transcription of judicial records, and care bestowed upon their compilation and preservation in rolls. Bracton, however, is the first writer who acknowledges the authority of such præjudicata, and lays down the decisions of the courts as leading authorities for the common law (*d*). As he himself avows, a great part of his matter was furnished by the "*vetera judicia justorum, facta ipsorum, consilia et responsa*," and the large number of cases cited in his work shows how much he owes to this source.

Judicial cases.

Bracton's use thereof.

When Bracton treats of rules of law which have always been recognized by ancient custom, it is of course evident that he has no need of quoting such authorities. Accordingly, we meet with citations of cases as precedents almost only when he is called upon to decide doubtful questions, or where he would demonstrate the origin and existence of principles of a special character, or of recent date. In this connection it is important to remember that the judicial decisions cited by Bracton are all, with one exception, of the reign of Henry III. (*e*), and belong to a period comparatively recent, the oldest thereof being of the year 1219, or 3 Henry III. It would be, however, too hazardous to conclude that the value of such decisions as legal authorities was not recognized in practice at an earlier period.

Dates of cases in Bracton.

(*d*) Bracton, 1 b. Si autem aliqua nova et inconsueta emerserint, et quæ prius usitata non fuerint in regno, si tamen *similia evenerint, per simile judicentur*, cum bona sit occasio a similibus procedere ad similia.

(*e*) This exception is a case *temp.* John, cited by Bracton, f. 364:—habetis de itinere M. de Pateshull in Com. Leycestriæ *de tempore regis Johannis.*

His manner of quoting and referring to them.

In quoting cases Bracton gives the year, term, and court. If the case occurred in eyre, the county, the judges and perhaps the sort of action are named (*f*). Usually he gives mere citations, but we often find added a more or less complete account of important matters of fact and law, which he generally takes from the rolls. The views of the judges are also often given,

---

(*f*) E.g.:—in assisis captis coram rege per Wilh. de Ralegh apud Cauteshull in comit. Norfolk anno regis H. 23, assisa novæ disseisinæ, si Robertus de Rikinghale.—It is not clear to me what years are meant by primis placitis *post guerram communem*, f. 77; anno secundo *post guerram*, f. 376 b.; and inter prima placita *post guerram*, f. 376 b. [If the true reading on fol. 77 is *guerram communem*, the phrase must have the same application as *guerram generalem* on fol. 240 b. The latter phrase can have no other application than to the civil war between John and the Barons, which broke out in the autumn of 1215, was raging at the death of John (19 October, 1216), and was terminated 11 September, 1217 (1 H. III.). This appears affirmatively and negatively from a record of 11 April, 1260: Rex etc. Deus......cum olim *guerra generalis* esset in Anglia, *nobis adhuc in minore aetate constitutis, imponi voluit regni diadema*, et ex insperato quos inimicitia capitalis ab invicem separaverat ad unitatem et pacem nostram dono suæ gratiæ revocavit, quam *toto tempore nostro sua gratia usque ad hæc tempora felicibus auspiciis continuavit* (Claus. Franc. 44 H. 3 in Prynne on 4 Inst. 154, 155). This may possibly have been called *guerra generalis* to distinguish it from the contest which had been terminated, or suspended, in June, 1215, by the pacification, or truce, of Runningmede, when Magna Charta was first granted. That contest was called a war in the convention between John and the Barons: omnes ex utraque parte recuperabunt castra terras et villas quas habuerunt in initio *guerræ*, ortæ inter dominum regem et barones. At this period, according to Wendover, the pleas of the Exchequer, and of the sheriffs' courts throughout England, ceased because there was no one who would account to the king, or in any wise obey him: cessaverunt placita scaccarii et Vicecomitum per Angliam quia nullus inventus est qui regi censum vel in aliquo obediret. This was then, and always afterwards, in England, the criterion of the definition of a time of internal war. The passages of Bracton with which to collate those here cited by the author, are on folios 16 b., 237 b., 238, 240, 302, 303 b., 313, 314 b., 373 b., 378, 390. Numerous entries in the printed close rolls of the latter part of the reign of John and early part of that of Henry III. show the character of the civil war at both of the periods above mentioned.

The foregoing remarks apply generally whether the phrase on fol. 77 is to be understood as guerram communem or simply guerram. Many passages of the context, proximate and immediate, might perhaps induce a doubt whether a slight corruption of the text has not misapplied the qualification communem to guerram instead of hæreditatem. The subject discussed is the communis hæreditas of parceners or female coheirs.—*Tr.*]

accompanied by a penetrating criticism and perhaps a censuring refutation (*g*). Bracton attributes particular importance to the opinions and decisions of certain judges, of whose ability we are also otherwise informed. These were Martin de Pateshull, William de Ralegh, Stephen de Segrave, the Abbot of Reading and the Bishop of Durham, who were much distinguished either as justices itinerant or as members of the court at Westminster (*h*). He appears to have cherished a special predilection for Martin de Pateshull, and it would seem from certain expressions that Bracton had personal relations with him (*i*). That no less authority was attributed to the responsa and consultationes of these judges than to their regular judicial decisions is to be inferred from repeated quotations (*j*).

Judges.

(*g*) Bracton, 50. 54 b. 82. 177. 199. 381 b. etc. *Differences of opinion:* 35 b.: Contrarium habetur de quadam abbatissa......coram W. de Ralegh, quod quidem S. de Segrave non approbavit; 130 b.: in quo casu diversæ fuerunt opiniones, et secundum M. de Pateshull...... Steph. de Segrave vero sentit contrarium. 438. *Censure* f. 29: contrarium factum fuit et *male de errore curiæ;* 49 b.: *male actum est in contrarium;* 277 b.: sed contrarium coram Rege et consilio suo apud Westm. anno regis H. 13.

(*h*) Martin de Pateshull was capitalis justiciarius de banco; William de Ralegh justiciarius domini regis; Stephen de Segrave, according to some expressions of Bracton, seems to have written upon tenant per legem Angliæ (tenant by courtesy). Bracton, 438: de consuetudine illa male intellecta et usitata. [Upon the above-named judges *cf.* Foss's Judges of England, II. 438, 448, 468.—*Tr.*]

(*i*) He calls him several times *dominus Martinus*, as well as merely Martinus. Bracton, 205 b. 207 b.: Melius secundum Martinum. [From Foss's account Martin de Pateshull was the most remarkable judge of his day.—*Tr.*]

(*j*) Bracton, 302 b.: Et unde P. de Rupe tunc Winton. episcopus *consuluit* eundem Martinum......qui *ei rescripsit* etc. F. 307: ad considerationem episcopi Wigorn. de *consilio Martini ex parte regis tale fuit datum responsum.* F. 357: ex responso W. de Ralegh et S. de Segrave facto Richardo Duket, *qui eorum consilium in hoc casu expetiit.* These responsa were not addressed to parties but to judges and persons exercising judicial functions of a subordinate and occasional character. [Most of the instances of consultations refer to cases of prohibition and the issue of writs of consultation, v. Reeves, I. 456. The writ of consultation on f. 307 did not, however, arise in a case of prohibition, v. note (*e*) to Chapter XVII. The case on f. 357 was one where the four knights, appointed to make a view in an essoin, were instructed as to their powers upon a doubted point. That the judges should define the powers of persons exercising under their supervision such occasional judicial functions, was a matter of course.—*Tr.*]

Use of Glanville discussed.

From the great consideration which Glanville's work enjoyed, it is doubtless to be presumed that Bracton was acquainted with it. The question next arises whether Bracton shows any traces of actually having used Glanville in composing his own book. A certain agreement in the prefaces of both works is not decisive, since it is clear that both authors have taken the prologue of Justinian's Institutes as a model (*k*). The difference between the general character of the two works is, indeed, opposed to the idea that the one should have materially affected or influenced the other. I can in fact point out only two passages (and those even without entire certainty) from which an immediate use of Glanville can be inferred; one, Lib. II. c. 26, which discusses testaments, seems to be taken from Glanville, VII. c. 5, and the other, Lib. II. c. 27, de emptionibus from Glanville, X. c. 14.

The statute of Merton, as I have already remarked, is expressly cited by Bracton in two passages (*l*).

ADDITIONAL NOTE TO CHAPTER III.

Bracton's references to recorded cases and his insertion of forms of writs are so numerous and so important that a detailed statement of them seems requisite.

Writs in Bracton.

The number of forms of writs, original and judicial, which Bracton gives, is 378. Besides these, there are suggestions of alternative forms of writs, which are not accompanied with the formal words to be substituted in the forms of writs to be altered, and which have not been included in the above aggregate.

(*k*) *Glanville:* Regiam potestatem non solum armis contra rebelles et gentes sibi regnoque insurgentes oportet esse decoratam sed et legibus ad subditos et populos pacifice regendos decet esse ornatam, ut utraque tempora pacis et belli etc.; *Bracton:* In rege, qui recte regit necessaria sunt duo hæc, arma videlicet et leges, quibus utrumque tempus bellorum et pacis recte possit gubernari.

(*l*) Bracton, 227, 416.

Detailed statement of cases in Bracton.

I have counted 484 cases in Bracton, making an average of about one to a folio. How often he cites a case more than once cannot be determined, for the citations are often too vague to enable the case to be identified without the roll, e.g. f. 260 b.: ut de itinere W. de Ralegh in comitatu Warr. assisa mortis antecessoris, circa medium rotuli. These cases are probably all with one exception of the reign of Henry III. That exception is the case on folio 364, de tempore regis Johannis, occurring before Pateshull in itinere in Leicestershire. Some other cases tried before Pateshull, which have no precise dates, may also have been of the reign of John. There are 353 cases dated by the years of the reign of Henry III.; 9 cases dated "post guerram," and one case "post guerram communem." There are 121 cases with no precise date, but in most instances the roll (generally that of an iter) can, if in existence, be identified from the reference.

The cases dated by the regnal years of Henry III. are as follows:

2 H. III., 3 cases; f. 239 (two), 308 b.

2 incipiente 3 H. III., 1 case; f. 409 b.

3 H. III., 25 cases; f. 23, 27 b., 50, 65, 113, 161, 200 b., 219, 277, 277 b., 280, 297, 298, 301 b., 303 b., 320 (two), 322, 330, 372, 375 b., 394 b., 421, 433, 442 b.

3 incipiente 4 H. III., 11 cases; f. 199 b., 243 b., 248 b., 258 b., 310, 316, 336, 413 b., 424 b., 437, 440 b.

4 H. III., 25 cases; f. 53, 93, 151 b., 199 b., 200, 200 b., 241 b., 272, 298, 305 b., 312, 319, 367, 375, 377 b., 387, 393 b., 414, 430 b. (two), 433 (two), 433 b., 436 b., 437 b.

4 incipiente 5 H. III., 4 cases; f. 65 b., 146, 387, 432 b.

5 H. III., 26 cases; f. 13, 54 b., 69, 83 b., 124 b., 128, 141, 153, 166, 179 b., 200 b., 246 b., 266 b., 269 b., 275 b., 286, 288 (two), 307 b., 332 b., 340 b., 375 b., 390, 430 b. (two), 433.

5 incipiente 6 H. III., 2 cases; f. 273, 311.

6 H. III., 12 cases; f. 53 b., 83, 245, 245 b., 246 b., 259 b., 350, 350 b., 351, 364, 407, 407 b.

6 incipiente 7 H. III., 3 cases; f. 143, 346, 420.

7 H. III., 19 cases; f. 55 b., 82, 93, 97 b., 141 b., 244, 306 b., 320 b., 349, 349 b., 351 b., 375 b., 376, 392 b., 407, 432 b., 433 b., 437, 437 b.

7 incipiente 8 H. III., 4 cases; 230 b., 311, 349, 350 b.

8 H. III., 13 cases; f. 29, 75, 246, 298, 306 b., 326 b., 387, 390 b., 392 b., 398 (two), 407, 414.

8 incipiente 9 H. III., 5 cases; f. 54 b., 212, 246, 298, 304.

9 H. III., 20 cases; f. 53 b. (two), 83, 84 b., 92, 142 b., 244 (two), 246, 246 b., 304 b., 316, 332 b., 364, 374, 390, 407, 434 (two), 436.

9 incipiente 10 H. III., 20 cases, f. 54 b., 84 b., 116 b., 137 b., 146, 146 b., 160 b., 246 b., 301 b., 304, 312, 344, 346, 355, 388 b., 423 b. (two), 430, 433 b., 440.

10 H. III., 25 cases; f. 54 b., 142 b., 212 b., 238 b. (two), 239, 246, 246 b., 260 b., 271 b., 275, 277 (two), 296 b., 304 b. (two), 306, 310, 340 b., 381, 408, 414, 418, 430 b., 438.

11 H. III., 3 cases; f. 239, 417, 421.

11 incipiente 12 H. III., 3 cases; f. 280 b., 418 b. (two).

12 H. III., 21 cases; f. 92 b., 148, 200, 205 b. (two), 226, 260, 261, 269 b., 274, 275 (two), 277, 285 b., 286, 288, 297, 371, 398, 413, 418, 433 b.

13 H. III., 8 cases; f. 27 b., 177, 200 (two), 225 b., 305 b., 348 b., 430 b.

13 incipiente 14 H. III., 2 cases; f. 315, 388 b.

14 H. III., 20 cases; f. 93, 226 b., 243 b., 297 b., 301, 319, 320, 339 b., 346 b., 350, 355 b., 356 b., 369 b., 374, 375, 391, 398, 415, 418, 437.

14 incipiente 15 H. III., 5 cases; f. 250, 297 b., 312, 379 b., 407 b.

15 H. III., 19 cases; f. 15, 29, 93, 130, 230 b., 286 b., 302 (two), 303, 316 b., 351 b., 384 b., 391 b., 407, 407 b. (two), 421, 423, 430, 436.

15 incipiente 16 H. III., 5 cases; f. 22, 343, 346, 359 b., 422 b.

16 H. III., 11 cases; f. 50 b., 341, 342 b. (two), 346, 367, 382, 392 b. (two), 407 b., 408.

16 incipiente 17 H. III., 4 cases; f. 50, 387, 422 b., 433.

17 H. III., 5 cases; f. 29, 87 b., 260, 298, 305 b.

18 H. III., 1 case; f. 230 b.

19 H. III., 2 cases; f. 16 b., 433 b.

20 H. III., 2 cases; f. 195, 317.

21 H. III., 5 cases; f. 31 b., 195, 272, 292 b., 298.

22 H. III., 1 case; f. 54 b.

23 H. III., 7 cases; f. 169 b., 195 (three), 200 (two), 368.

24 H. III., 2 cases; f. 293 b., 373.

30 H. III., 5 cases; f. 413, 414, 414 b., 423, 436.

31 H. III., 1 case; f. 414.

32 H. III., 1 case; f. 234 b.

32 incipiente 33 H. III., 1 case; f. 241.

38 H. III., 1 case; f. 339 b.

46 H. III., 1 case; f. 159.

The cases dated "post guerram" are as follows:

Itinere......post guerram de loquelis quæ remanserunt ad judicium, 1 case; f. 390.

Inter prima placita post guerram, 1 case; f. 376 b. If the reading post guerram communem be corrupt, there should be here added the case on f. 77 in rotulo de primis placitis post guerram communem.

2 H. III. post guerram, 5 cases; f. 313, 314 b., 376 b., 378 b., 380. Anno secundo post guerram, 1 case; f. 378. In secundo rotulo post guerram, 1 case; f. 302.

The 121 other cases are to be found on f. 16 b., 20, 23, 26, 27, 28, 29, 35 b., 45, 49 b., 50 (three), 56 b., 65, 88 b., 95 b., 114, 125 b., 128, 130 b., 137, 142 b., 144 b., 146 b., 167, 169, 170, 170 b., 188, 199 (three), 199 b. (three), 200 b., 205 b. (two), 212 (two), 226, 226 b., 239, 244 b. (two), 246, 247 b., 260 b., 266 b., 270 b., 271 (two), 271 b., 272 (three), 272 b., 273 b. (two), 274 (three), 275, 276 b. (two), 277, 277 b. (two), 278 (three), 280, 280 b. (two), 285, 285 b. (two), 286, 290 b., 296, 297 b., 304, 309 (two), 311, 312 (two), 319, 320, 320 b., 330 b., 340 b., 343, 350 (three), 350 b. (three), 357, 370 b., 377 b., 381 (two), 381 b., 383, 388, 390, 390 b., 393 b., 398, 417 b., 418, 420, 420 b., 421 b., 422 b. (two), 424, 426, 426 b., 427 b., 430 b., 435 b., 438.

The great mass of these cases without precise date were tried before either Martin de Pateshull or William de Ralegh, or both, with or without associates. The former died in 1229, and the latter appears to have been off the bench after 1235, 19 Henry III.; see Foss, II. 440, 449.

To these should be added Bracton's references on f. 93 b., 130 b., 141, 194 b., 292, 306 b., 307, 309, 310 b., 422 b., most of which are undoubted citations of cases. On f. 320 b. there is evidently an omitted case.

Judges' opinions are cited on f. 130 b., 183, 205 b., 207 b., 330, 374, 438.—*Translator.*

CHAPTER IV.

FOREIGN SOURCES AND AUTHORITIES—ROMAN LAW.

Foreign sources.

Roman law.

THE elements of law of foreign origin, which are found in Bracton, are derived from the Roman and Canon laws. The former, however, furnishes the greater and most important part. I reserve for the Second Part of this treatise the detailed investigation of Bracton's Roman matter. I will at present only speak of the manner and the extent of the use of the Roman law and of its general importance in Bracton's work.

Roman law in Glanville.

Traces of an acquaintance with the Roman law are indeed seen in Glanville, but an actual use of it can only be demonstrated in his discussion of agreements and contracts in the tenth book (*a*). On the other hand, no small part of Bracton's matter is derived from the Roman law. And, while the Roman is treated as a foreign law by Glanville, and the opposition of the "*leges Romanæ*" to the "*consuetudo regni*" is often put forward, the case is far different with Bracton. In the latter's work the Roman law no longer appears as a stranger, nor as a merely tolerated element of the law, but as one which in rank and origin is equal to the Common law. Thus, in Bracton we find a terminology which is either borrowed from the Roman law or conceived in its forms. We meet with Roman legal maxims which have become proverbial, and

In Bracton's work.

(*a*) The tenth book of Glanville is entitled: de debitis laicorum, in contradistinction to those matters of debt in which remedies were only to be obtained in the courts Christian. In it are treated *causa mutui* cum quis credit alii aliquid quod consistit in numero, pondere et mensura; *causa depositi; causa commodati* ut si rem meam tibi gratis commodem ad usum; *causa emptionis*, and *locati conducti*. There is also much borrowed from the Roman law in regard to *plegiorum datio*. [*Cf.* Reeves, I. 159, note (*u*); Cortelyou v. Lansing, 2 Caines's Cases, 204, 212.—*Tr.*]

seem to be naturalized in England, as for instance: pater est quem nuptiæ demonstrant; melior est conditio possidentis; scienti et volenti non fit injuria; expressa nocent, non expressa non nocent; cessante causa, cessat effectus; modus et conventio vincunt legem, etc. More than this, in many branches of the law we find legal principles and notions which are derived or borrowed from the Roman law; here in slight traces, there in the full force of a transplantation of the whole Institutes from the Corpus Juris to the soil of England; sometimes standing isolated in sharp relief beside the domestic law, sometimes at the very moment of amalgamation with it, transforming and completing it.

In Bracton's system.

This influence of the Roman law is equally seen in Bracton's system. As has been before observed, the first part of his system is planned after the tripartite division of Justinian's Institutes. This reproduction of the system of the Institutes goes also into details; *not* indeed so far as Biener thinks (*b*), who, at the expense of our author's originality, asserts that the greatest part of the Institutes is worked into Bracton's book. It is in fact no great part of them at all, for the imitation does not exceed the following limits: Bracton's first book corresponds to the Institutes I. Tit. 1–4, 8, 9, and 12; chapters 1–4 of his second book correspond to the first two titles of the second book of the Institutes; and chapters 1–4 of the first tract of his third book follow in general the course of the Institutes III. Tit. 13–15, 18, 19, 29 and IV. Tit. 6. In the Second Part, this will appear more fully in detail. *Moreover, Bracton can claim the order and arrangement of his matter as original. In this respect he is indeed superior to his contemporary Civilian brethren, who in their commentaries upon the law followed the written order of the Roman authorities without as yet having arrived at any original systematic treatment of the law of their own* (1).

Bracton has taken the Roman law partly from the original

(*b*) Inq. Pr. 221.

(1) The translator has italicised this remark, which from its importance deserves special attention.—*Tr.*

authorities, and partly has used secondary treatises. His acquaintance with the Corpus Juris and his actual use of it, are proved by a series of quotations expressly made therefrom. These are sometimes *mere citations*, and sometimes embrace the texts themselves, and are of course occasionally much disfigured by clerical errors. The Novels are not quoted, and probably were not used. The Institutes are expressly mentioned in one passage only, where they are referred to as a whole (*c*). On the other hand, I have discovered twelve express quotations from the Digest and ten from the Code, the particulars of which are given in the note below (*d*). The method

His use of the Corpus Juris.

List of his express quotations from the Corpus Juris.

(*c*) Bracton, 10.: *ut in Institutis......plenius inveniri poterit.*

(*d*) I. Quotations from the Digest. (The quotations from the Corpus Juris are given as they are found in Bracton.)

1. Bracton, f. 12 b. lex F. de donationibus, post contractum crimen, and f. 30 b. F. de donation. L. post contractum = L. 15. D. 39. 5.

2. f. 113. ff. ad *legem Juliani* (sic) de vi publica, lege si de vi = L. 5. § 1. D. 48. 6.

3. f. 114. F. quod metus causa L. *similiter si coactus* (evidently instead of L. si mulier § si coactus) = L. 21. § 1. D. 4. 2.

4. ibid. C. (must mean F.) de tribut. actione L. quod in heredem § eligere = L. 9. § 1. D. 14. 4.

5. ibid. F. quorum legatorum L. prima = L. 1. § 4. D. 43. 3.

6. ibid. F. *locari* (instead of locati) L. si merces § culpæ nomine = L. 25. § 4. D. 19. 2.

7. ibid. F. de act. et oblig. ss. *si servum* (instead of: qui servum) = L. 34. pr. D. 44. 7.

8. 114 b. F. *de pullicianis* (sic!) et *vectigalibus* L. interdum § pœnæ = L. 16. § 13. D. 39. 4.

9. f. 128 b. F. ad legem Jul. de sicariis et veneficiis ubi dicitur, quod transfuges ubicunque inventi etc. = L. 3. § 6. D. 48. 8.

10. f. 129. F. de requirend. reis L. ultima = L. 5. D. 48. 17.

11. f. 152. F. de pœna (pœnis) L. pregnantis = L. 3. D. 48. 19.

12. f. 410 b. ff. ad *legem Julianam* (sic!) de adulteriis, lege denunciasse C. *quære* (must mean: § quæritur) = L. 17. § 6. D. 48. 5.

I am not able to find the quotation on f. 114: F. de privatis delictis L. non utique.

II. Quotations from the Code:

1. f. 16 b. C. de pactis, in bonæ fidei contr. = L. 13. C. 2. 3.

2. f. 29 b. C. de donat. ante nuptias L. cum *milite* (instead of: cum multæ) = L. 20. C. 5. 3.

3. f. 106 b. C. ad legem Vel (instead of: Jul.) *de repet.* L. omnis = L 3. C. 9. 27.

4. ibid. C. ss (i.e. eod.) L. ultima = L. 6. C. 9. 27.

of citation presents nothing peculiar. Much greater, however, is the number of passages of the Roman law, which are incorporated into the text itself, and into the tissue of the author's commentary *without any statement of their source.* These include not only particular *leges*, but also whole connected fragments of the Corpus Juris reproduced in an order but slightly modified (*e*).

But the original authorities of the Roman law themselves have been less used by Bracton than a secondary treatise, which in his time enjoyed a great reputation. This was the well-known *Summa* of Azo *to the Code* and *to the Institutes*, the wide dissemination of which beyond the limits of Italy is thus proved by its use in England. This work of the renowned Glossator (*f*) seems to have ex-

His use of Azo.

5. f. 114. C. de *heredibus* (must mean: de hereditatis petitione) L. cogi possessorem = L. 11. C. 3. 31.

6. f. 114 b. C. de injuriis L. ult. = L. 11. C. 9. 35.

7. f. 128 b. C. de iis qui latrones et malef. occultant L. prima = L. 1. C. 9. 39.

8. f. 129. C. de requir. reis L. quicunque = L. 2. C. 9. 40.

9. f. 183 b. C. de edendo L. qui accusari = L. 4. C. 2. 1.

10. ibid. C. de rei vindicatione L. penultima = L. 27. C. 3. 32., as L. ultima: res alienas possidens etc., must be meant. [D. de adq. poss. 41. 2. is referred to generally on f. 16, —ut dicetur plenius in titulo de adquirenda possessione.—*Tr.*]

(*e*) Thus we find on f. 43 b. a great part of L. 1. §§ 2–15 D. de adquir. poss. 41. 2.; f. 99 b. much taken from Inst. 3. 13 *sq.*; f. 162. 162 b. L. 3. §§ 2–11 D. de vi 43. 16.; f. 233. L. 1 § 2 *sq.* D. de rivis 43, 21, etc.

(*f*) Upon Azo: v. Savigny, Gesch., V. 1–44. The Summæ of the Code and of the Institutes are intended by Azo to be *one work.* I have used and cited in this treatise the following edition: Lugduni, apud Joan. et Francisc. Frellæos, 1540. ["Azo ou Azolinus, né a Bologne, ou il mourut en 1230. Disciple de Joannes Bassianus, il acquit une grande reputation, bien qu'il y ait de l'exagération de la part de ses biographes, qui ont dit qu'il avait dix mille auditeurs a son cours et qu'il le donnait sur la place publique...... Les ecrits d'Azo jouirent d'une reputation *qui eclipsa celle de tous ses devanciers*, et les tribunaux lui accordèrent un tel credit que pour obtenir une place de juge, il fallait posseder la *somme* d'Azo. De là ce proverbe: *Chi non ha Azzo—non vada a Palazzo.* Ses principaux ouvrages sont ses gloses sur les cinq parties du *Corpus Juris Civilis*, ses *Lecturæ* et son *Apparatus in Codicem*, ses *Brocarda*, ses *Quæstiones*, et ce qui a valu le plus de célébrité, sa *Summa* du Code et des Institutes, dont il a été imprimé plus de trente editions." Eschbach, Introduction Generale à l'étude du Droit, p. 264. Upon the Glossators, *cf.* Hallam, Literature, I. 62; Mackeldey's Civil Law englished by Kaufmann, I. 66 *sq.*; Lindley's Introduction to Jurisprudence, Appendix, p. viii.—*Tr.*]

erted an important influence upon the design, if not upon the origin, of Bracton's work, and to have served him as a model. Like Azo, Bracton calls the dogmatic exposition of the law of his nation a *summa* ("in unam summam redigendo") (*g*). His introduction discusses and explains the design, purpose, and utility of his work, and the reader may see from the extracts in the note how much they agree with those of Azo (*h*). There is, however, the most marked contrast between the simple modesty of Bracton's introduction and the immoderate tone of the renowned but pretentious Italian (*i*). This modesty and his concurrence in the general high opinion of the merit of Azo's work, serve to explain why Bracton has used it so extensively. Throughout nearly the whole of Bracton's book, we can distinctly trace the scientific influence of Azo's views and doctrines, especially in the definitions and divisions of legal notions and conceptions, which are generally clothed in Azo's words.

(*g*) Bracton, f. 1.

(*h*) Bracton, 1 b. *Intentio* autem autoris est......docere et instruere omnes qui edoceri desiderant, qualiter et quo ordine lites decidantur secundum leges et consuetudines Anglicanas......ut doceantur et corrigantur errantes, puniantur contumaces. Item communis intentio est de jure scribere, ut rudes efficiantur boni, et boni meliores tum metu pœnarum, tum exhortatione præmiorum.

......*Finis* hujus rei est, ut sopiantur jurgia et vitia propulsentur et ut in regno pax conservetur et justitia. Ethicæ vero supponitur quasi morali scientiæ, quia tractat de moribus.

Azo in Inst. prol. f. 239 b. *Intentio* communis est......quemadmodum lites decidantur, doceantur errantes, puniantur contumaces. Item est communis intentio de jure rescribere, et adeo rescribendo operam dare, ut homines mali efficiantur boni, et boni efficiantur meliores tum metu pœnarum, tum exhortatione præmiorum.

Ad hunc *finem* referuntur omnes conditores, ut jurgia sint sopita et expulsa sint vitia...... Ethicæ supponitur liber iste, quia tractat de moribus.

(*i*) Azo in Codic Proem. Nunc autem......honorabilium sociorum precibus condescendi......juxta ipsorum amicabiles supplicationes......summas lucide tractare studebo...... Suscipiatis ergo......lucidum et favorabile munus, quod a me diutius postulastis, tenentes, quod nihil *obscurum nihil dubitabile, nihilque contrarium legibus* invenietis.

Compare Bracton's address to the reader: postulans ut si quid superfluum vel perperam positum in hoc opere invenerit, illud corrigat vel emendet, vel conniventibus oculis pertranseat, cum omnia habere in memoria et in nullo peccare divinum sit potius quam humanum.

Cf. also Savigny, V. 28.

Bracton has, however, gone still farther in availing himself of Azo's assistance, farther indeed than is consistent with our present notions of an author's dignity. Particularly where Bracton follows the course of the Institutes, that is to say, in his exposition of the law of persons, of the division and modes of acquiring things, and of the law of actions, he generally does not lay down the text of the original authority as a foundation, but gives unaltered Azo's corresponding commentary in his Summa of the Institutes, merely omitting his citations and making necessary abbreviations and changes; or, to speak more precisely, he transcribes whole pages literally (*j*).

We must not, however, look upon Bracton as an author who could not rise above the level of a mere plagiarist, an opinion to which his contemporaries would never have given their assent (*k*). That he was equal to his task of giving a dogmatic exposition of the English law, is shown by the no small part of his work in which he stands upon his own feet, and makes proof of his capacity without assistance from others. Putting aside personal predilection, the real reason for Bracton's copying Azo so closely, seems to have been the general diffusion and high reputation which Azo's works had obtained in England as well as elsewhere within the thirty years following his death (*l*). Their superiority to the earlier text books and works of similar scope may have led

---

(*j*) This applies even to the most marked peculiarities, e.g. Azo, 241, remarks: *tabellio* qui dicitur servus publicus a serviendo derivari potest; so too Bracton, 4 b. Azo, 246 b., enumerates calodæmones, cacodæmones, et animæ hominum among res incorporales, which Bracton does also, f. 10. [In Bracton's day, to copy what was deemed useful, was not considered plagiarism. Numerous proofs might be adduced to show that there was then no feeling resembling the Roman or the modern delicacy upon this subject. In Chapter V. the author remarks that where Bracton seems as it were to copy the Roman law, he does not leave us in any doubt that he is laying it down as English law and only as such, in some places by interpolating a word or making a slight addition, in others by an omission or alteration of what does not conform to the Common law. The parallel extracts from Bracton and Azo, which are given in Chapter XII., enable the reader to see how carefully Bracton modified Azo, when it was necessary to do so.—*Tr.*]

(*k*) *Cf.* Savigny, Gesch. III. 574.

(*l*) Savigny, V. 7. 8.—Azo died in 1230.

in England, as we know it did in Italy (*m*), to their being to a certain extent preferred to the original sources for immediate practical use even in the Courts. If Azo's writings had thus become elevated to a sort of original authority, it does not seem strange that Bracton should have preferred to take the Roman law applicable in England (*n*) in its then most generally accepted form of Azo's commentary, nor that he should have incorporated parts of the latter's writings in his own work. How generally Azo was known and used in England, is plainly shown by a passage of Bracton, which directly refers the reader to Azo's writings for further details (*o*).

Use of other writers discussed.

It appears to me improbable that Bracton used any other writer upon the Roman law than Azo. I have compared *Placentin's* (²) Summa of the Institutes and Code upon the principal points, and have found only one passage to which any resemblance can be supposed, and even in that case it is doubtful. A remark of Bracton's, f. 99, is to this effect: est enim obligatio *quasi contra ligatio.* This may be connected with Placentin's describing obligatio as *quasi ligatio* (ad Inst. 3. 12), for Azo does not use this expression. I have not been able to find any traces of Bracton's acquaintance with the well-known work of *Magister Vacarius*, the Liber ex universo enucleato Jure excerptus (³), as far as I have examined a manuscript of it. It seems in Bracton's time to have become almost superseded by the writings of the Italian school.

Biener's doubt (in Savigny, IV. 586), whether the exposition (f. 99 *sq.*) of the law of obligations and particularly that

(*m*) Upon the use of Azo's writings in the Courts, see Savigny, V. 11.

(*n*) For evidence of the application of Roman law in England, see the following Chapter.

(*o*) Bracton, f. 10. ut in Institutis plenius inveniri poterit *et in summa Azonis.*

(²) Placentin died in 1192, in France, where he had filled the first professorial chair, which was established in that country for teaching the Civil law. *Cf.* Eschbach, Introduction, p. 268; Kaufmann's Mackeldey, I. 70, 66.—*Tr.*

(³) Upon Vacarius, *cf.* the able article in the Penny Cyclopædia by a writer familiar with what has been written in Germany concerning him; Kaufmann's Mackeldey, I. 71 *sq.*—*Tr.*

of stipulations, is to be regarded as *Bracton's own work*, is removed by the manifest fact that the Institutes III. tit. 15–18 were immediately used in preparing it. Biener also doubts the originality of some of the examples mentioned in Bracton, such as, "do tibi codicem, ut des mihi digestum," etc. This doubt in my opinion is founded upon an underrating of Bracton's acquaintance with the Roman law. It can hardly be thought remarkable that a writer, the whole contents of whose work show such close familiarity with the Corpus Juris, should have invented such examples in addition to those which he has borrowed from it.

CHAPTER V.

IMPORTANCE OF THE ROMAN LAW IN BRACTON.

Opinions concerning the Roman law in Bracton.

THE frequent use which Bracton has made of the Roman law has sometimes subjected him to the reproach of having favored it at the expense of the domestic law. In consequence of this alleged Romanizing tendency he has occasionally been refused recognition as a true and genuine source and authority for English law. Houard, the French editor of the early English law books, has in particular endeavored to maintain this and many other strange propositions in his *Traités sur les Coutumes Anglo-Normandes*, and has on this account taken occasion to exclude Bracton from his collection (*a*). These attacks upon Bracton are, however, altogether unfounded, and Reeves and after him Biener have decisively refuted them. But there is another erroneous view which is connected with this mistaken estimate of Bracton, namely, that of underrating the importance of the Roman law in Bracton and for the English law of his time. Upon this latter question, there is, indeed, a diversity of opinions. Reeves considers the Roman law in Bracton to be merely an external ornament, and an embellishment of scientific learning (*b*). Biener is of opinion that Bracton accords to the Roman law no legislative authority, but only that of a naturalis ratio. Spence, on the other hand, holds the Roman law in our author's work to be good and valid law, incorporated into the common

Reeves's view.

Biener's view.

Spence's view.

(*a*) *Cf.* Biener, Engl. Geschw. Ger. II. 287 *sq.*, upon Houard. [*Cf.* Reeves, II. 88 note, 283 note.—*Tr.*]

(*b*) Reeves, II. 88: "Upon a second consideration of those places where the Roman law is stated with most confidence, it will seem to be rather alluded to for illustration and ornament, than adduced as an authority." This view is hardly reconcilable with what is said II. 54.

law (*c*). My own investigations have led me to adopt a view, which is essentially the same as that of Spence. The external historical evidence as well as the internal evidence of Bracton's work itself, demonstrate that no inconsiderable part of the Roman law must have been practically applied in England in Bracton's day. The same evidence also shows that Bracton has *in general* (*d*) given a place to, and reproduced, only those Roman elements which he found were in England actually valid law (i.e. such as were actually *received*).

View here maintained.

We must above all recollect the circumstances under which Bracton wrote. His purpose was of a purely practical character, namely, to lay down the English law for *English judges* merely, and to explain and to teach "qualiter et quo ordine lites decidantur *secundum leges et consuetudines Anglicanas.*" His materials were purely English materials: "facta et casus, qui quotidie emergunt et eveniunt in *regno Angliæ*" (*e*). His sources and authorities were equally English, being English judicial decisions, and rules of law which were applied or were to be applied by English courts. Recollecting these facts we are at a loss to explain why Bracton should have mentioned the Roman law at all, if it was indeed an utterly foreign law, or if it had obtained no footing in the legal soil of England. Still less under such circumstances, can we explain why he should have made use of the Roman law to the extent to which he did. He could not have done so for the judges, for they would have had no need of it, nor for students, for they would get a better idea of it from the Corpus Juris itself, or from the law schools. Moreover, the manner in which Brac-

Discussion of the Roman law in Bracton.

(*c*) Biener, in Savigny, IV. 585, relies especially upon the following passage in Bracton's preface: cum autem in fere omnibus regionibus utantur legibus et *jure scripto*, sola Anglia usa est in suis finibus jure non scripto et consuetudine. Jus scriptum is here taken to mean the *Roman law*. Biener subsequently concedes that much use was made of the Roman law in the highest courts in England both in Glanville's and in Bracton's time. *Cf.* Biener Englische Geschwornengericht, II. 265. Spence, I. 123. 124. 131. 235.

(*d*) I say in general, for I will not deny that in particular instances Bracton has himself made additions.

(*e*) Bracton, 1 b.

ton discusses and treats the Roman law is decisively in favor of the view here maintained. There is no difference to be observed in his commentary, whether he is dwelling upon English or upon Roman principles. He passes over both alike. The reader, instead of getting the impression that sometimes domestic and sometimes foreign materials are presented to him, finds before him the picture of an indivisible homogeneous whole, in which the Roman elements are *no longer merely Roman law*, but have become integral parts of the *leges et consuetudines Anglicanæ* (*f*). This sort of commentary cannot be reconciled with the supposition that Roman law has been merely introduced by the writer as an external addition and for the sake of elegance; it can only be justified when the Roman law in exactly the way in which it had been adopted, was fully entitled to its place in his commentary as naturalized valid law. Bracton, himself a judge and a writer scrupulously cautious of giving his assent to doubtful propositions, was not the man to have left his reader in doubt as to what he considered *law*, and what *mere ornament.* His work bears throughout the stamp of the author's fidelity to truth, but a great part of it would belie such a character, and he would himself be subjected to the charge of having falsified the law, if it be true that he has laid down Roman as English law for whole pages without any reserve.

The confident and matter-of-course way in which Bracton takes it for granted that there is no necessity for giving the Roman authorities, or when he does cite them, uses the same "ad hoc facit" with which he quotes English cases (*g*), together with the circumstance that in particular instances he even adduces English precedents (*h*) for Roman principles, prove that he was remarkably careful in the application of

---

(*f*) The instances given in the Second Part make this evident.

(*g*) E.g. Bracton, 16, 16 b. 128 b. 129 *et al.* The Roman law is often called by Bracton *lex* merely; e.g. 20 b., convenit *lex* cum consuetudine Anglicana; f. 130., quia dicit *lex;* f. 150 b., furtum est secundum *leges* contrectatio rei alienæ, etc., where this definition is, without any explanation being added, presumed as a matter of course to be English law; *leges Romanæ* are only mentioned f. 147 b. where they are placed in opposition to the *leges* Francorum.

(*h*) Bracton, 29, for the prohibition of donationes inter conjuges; and f. 113.

Roman law. The Roman law is not of uniform importance throughout, as might be expected, if it were merely added as an external ornament, or if it were only recognized as a higher authority by the author's caprice. Instead of this, in a number of subjects we find only single Roman principles of isolated application, and in many others, exactly where the Roman law is nearest at hand, we meet with no traces of its influence. Thus when Bracton mentions some general principles upon the subject of the patria potestas, he gives none of the characteristic peculiarities of that Roman institution. In discussing usucapio (a thing manifestly borrowed from the Roman law) he altogether rejects the Digest with its rich materials, while just before he makes the most extended use of it for the doctrine of possession. Concerning testaments we find hardly anything said reminding us of the Roman law, and there are but scant traces of it in what is laid down concerning emptio, locatio, etc. Such instances as these cannot certainly be attributed to mere accident (*i*). So far from going unnecessarily into the Roman law, Bracton avoids doing so throughout, because it was his wish and his duty to reproduce only such Roman law as was of practical validity in England, and because all else did not belong to an exposition of the leges et consuetudines Angliæ (*j*). Bracton, too, where he seems, as it were, to copy the Roman law, does not leave us in any doubt that he is laying it down as *English law and only as such;* in some places by interpolating a word, or making a slight addition, in others by an omission or alteration of what does not conform to the Common law (*k*). Hence the errors or mistakes concerning the

(*i*) *Cf.* the Second Part. The number of these examples could be much augmented.

(*j*) That they were not much inclined in England to sacrifice the domestic to the foreign law, is proved by the stubborn opposition to the Roman-Canonical legitimatio per subsequens matrimonium. The frankness with which Bracton takes the part of the English custom in the controversy, justifies us in thinking that he would not in other cases arbitrarily favor the foreign at the expense of the domestic law.

(*k*) E.g. Bracton, 4, *jus civile* quod dici potuit *jus consuetudinarium;* f. 5, the modification through villenage of the maxim "partus sequitur ventrem;" f. 6 b, si damnetur propter aliquam feloniam, instead of, si damnetur in metallum vel

Roman law which are found in his work, are specially important. To make Bracton responsible for them would be most unjustly accusing him of gross ignorance (*l*), and we therefore can only suppose that he has incorporated them into his work because they were actually current in the legal views of the day. These errors are hence no small guaranty for the fidelity to truth of Bracton's exposition of the law, and besides furnish proof that upon particular points Roman elements had begun to amalgamate with those of the Common law.

English medieval law books following Bracton.

Finally, the force of the foregoing arguments is much strengthened by taking into consideration the important influence which Bracton exercised upon the writers on the English law who succeeded him (*m*). They take Bracton as a model without at all rejecting his Roman law as an arbitrary addition. On the contrary, they reproduce it entire. In their opinion, therefore, Bracton used it and laid it down as valid English law.

Force of the Roman law in England.

Of course we must not imagine that the Roman law had any *legislative* authority in England. The application and adoption of Roman legal principles was in England no more connected with a legislative authority of the Corpus Juris than it was in Germany during the period of *reception* or adoption. The consequent *reception* (if I may use such a term) of the Roman law in England, which was indeed but of a limited character, was there as in Germany an act of the consuetudinary law.

Causes thereof.

Many causes combined to open the way for the practical application of Roman law. Among

---

opus metalli, in Azo 242 b.; Bracton, 8 b., the *subsidiary* application of the Roman law in regard to occupatio—nisi consuetudo se habeat in contrarium; the exclusion of the Roman theory of treasure trove — propter fisci (*regis*) privilegium. So also f. 9 b. as to islands in flumine *publico*.—Etc.

(*l*) Thus, f. 16, he bases the necessity of a traditio to perfect a donatio upon the maxim, ex nudo pacto non oritur actio; f. 29, although the English donatio was altogether different from the Roman, he applies the Roman prohibition of donationes inter conjuges to the former; although dos in the English law was altogether different from the Roman institution of that name, he divides it into dos adventitia and dos profectitia; he calls the forisfamiliation of children, emancipatio.

(*m*) Upon these writers, see Chapter VII.

these were the impulse given by the universities and the Oxford School of Civil Law (*n*), the recognition of the Roman law in the clerical courts whose jurisdiction extended over a class of civil matters (*o*), and the personal influence of the higher judges who mostly belonged to the clergy and were therefore versed in the Roman law (*p*). Above all, however, was the necessity of supplying the defects of the Common law, which had become manifest from the growth of trade, the increase of intercourse, and the greater importance of movable property; for the Common law had expended its best energies in the completion of the legal constitution of the feudal system and had showed no tendency towards creating an original commercial law (*q*). To these causes must also be added the scientific superiority of the foreign law with its completeness, over the domestic law with its want of theoretical development (*r*). Even at an earlier

(*n*) *Cf.* Savigny Gesch. d. R. R. IV. 429; Duck, De Usu et Auctoritate Juris Civilis; 365 *sq.* 404 *sq.* [*Cf.* Spence, I. 109.—*Tr.*]

(*o*) The ecclesiastical jurisdiction had a more extended sphere of operation in England than elsewhere. It not only extended to what were properly causæ spirituales (as matrimonial causes, spiritual offenses), but also to testaments, to successions ab intestato of movable property, to legitimacy, and even to agreements or contracts as far as their violation came within ecclesiastical censure as læsio or transgressio fidei. It is not improbable that the Romanisms, which occur in Glanville's explanation of contracts, found their way into the Curia Regis from the Courts Christian, as they were called. *Cf.* Reeves, I. 63–81. Phillips, Eng. Rechtsgeschichte, I. 165; II. 69, 209 and elsewhere. Stephen, Comment. on the Eng. Laws, IV. 1–18; Duck, De Usu, 599 *sq.* Henry II. had vainly contended against the extension of the ecclesiastical jurisdiction in his Constitutions of Clarendon (1164).

(*p*) Almost all the chancellors, as well as most of the judges of the higher courts were clerks; M. de Pateshull, decanus St. Pauli; W. Ralegh, clericus. Besides the Abbot of Reading and the episcopus Dunelmensis, Bracton mentions Radulf. episcop. Cistrensis, and the episcop. Carliensis as judges.

(*q*) See Goldschmidt's Archiv für das gesammte Handelsrecht, IV. 13 *sq.* for an essay upon "The History of Commercial Law in England," in which I have attempted to show, as far as commercial law is concerned, how much the wants and necessities of the period assisted the *reception* of foreign rules of law.

(*r*) Perhaps here too reference should be made to a certain internal similarity between the judicial and remedial machinery of the English and that of the Roman law, to which Biener has called attention in Mittermeyer's krit. Zeitschrift, XIX. 167 *sq.* But it might be difficult to demonstrate in detail the operation of this force upon the adoption of Roman principles.

period it is not improbable that the Roman law had been used as an assistant and complementary authority in the Curia Regis, upon which court it was incumbent to instruct the inferior judges in regard to the law in doubtful and omitted cases (*s*). A legal principle enunciated by that court had authority beyond the particular case in which it was laid down, and became by means of its actual use, part of the jus non scriptum, consuetudinarium. *As Roman legal matter obtained reception, although the written sources of the Roman law were not at all received as having a legislative authority*, Bracton properly included the former among the leges et consuetudines Angliæ (*t*) ([1]).

Curia Regis.

(*s*) Bracton, 1 b. Si autem talia (similia) nunquam prius evenerint et obscurum vel difficile sit eorum judicium, tunc ponantur judicia in respectum ad magnam Curiam, ut ibi *per consilium Curiæ* terminentur. *Cf.* note (*d*), Chapter III.

(*t*) The passage quoted in note (*c*) above, upon which Biener lays so much stress, does not therefore conflict at all with our view. Moreover, Bracton himself says just after: habent enim Anglici plurima ex consuetudine, quæ non habent ex lege, and thereby somewhat restricts his previous remark.

([1]) In connection with the subject of this chapter, compare the author's remarks in the beginning of Chapter XII. Bracton seems to have been of opinion that the Roman jurisprudence, as that of all Christendom, was in force in England, as a jus naturale or jus gentium, except where supplied or displaced by general or local English usages or by English Constitutions (statutes).—*Tr.*

CHAPTER VI.

CANON LAW.

THE use of the Canon law in Bracton is far more restricted than that of the Roman law. The *Decretum* is cited on f. 114 b.: Canon law in Bracton.

> "et illustres personæ injuriarum per procuratores agere possunt ut III. Q. IX. in fine;" Quotations from the Decretum.

this is evidently the dictum Gratiani in c. 18. Caus. III. qu. 9. The sigla, on f. 183 b., V. Q. V. C. I. must also be a corrupted quotation of the Decretum, although I have not been able to find the exact passage (*a*).

On f. 63 the following is quoted *verbatim* from the *Decretals*, c. 2. X. qui filii. 4. 17: From the Decretals.

> "et ad hoc facit decretale, cujus verba hæc sunt: inter J. virum et V. mulierem," etc.

Immediately before this passage is an extract from c. 3. X. de cland. desp. 4. 3.; whether it is made from the compilation of Gregory IX. or some one older, cannot be decided. Besides these authorities Bracton mentions in several places the provision of the Lateran Council of 1179 (*temp.* Alexander III.) concerning filling vacant churches while the right of patronage was in dispute (*b*). That the Canon law was not, indeed, without influence upon the English law, can be seen from the many traces we find of it in Bracton. The exposition of the right of patron- Influence of the Canon law upon the English.

(*a*) The citation is made by the side of: L. 4. Cod. 2. 1. and L. 28. Cod. 3. 32.

(*b*) Bracton, 241. 247. 334; "Constitutio Lateranensis de ecclesiis vacantibus;" *cf.* c. 3. and 22 X. de jur. patron. 3. 38. It is here worthy of remark

age (*advocatio*) and of the assise connected with it (*assisa ultimæ præsentationis*), reproduces the provisions of different decretals (*c*). The Criminal law also contains many things taken from the Canon law, as for instance in the proceeding per famam patriæ (*d*), and in the law of homicide (*e*). In procedure the influence of the Canon law is unmistakable in the wager of law, in proof by charters, in the proof of charters by witnesses (*f*), in the challenges of the jurata (*g*), in the exceptio spoliationis (*h*), and in the *præsumptio ex semiplena probatione* mentioned in one passage (*i*). In the law of inheritance the computation of the degrees of kindred, and the recognition of the right of representation are to be referred to the influence of the Canon law (*j*).

But the influence of the Canon law, at least before Bracton's time, was in general less important than we might be led to expect after the advantages gained by the Church in Henry the Second's reign and that king's abortive attempt at emancipation, followed by John's complete submission to Innocent III. The papal supremacy seems, indeed, to have been used more for the extension of the clerical jurisdiction, and for arbitrary encroachments

Clerical jurisdiction in England.

---

that Bracton speaks only of the term of six months and not of that of four. Must it therefore be inferred that the distinction between lay and clerical patronage which was usual elsewhere did not obtain in England?

(*c*) Bracton, 238–252. Most of the Decretals in the title de jur. patron. (c. 5. 6. 7–11. 19–21. X. 3. 38) are addressed to England, and portions of them can only be understood by a knowledge of the English matters to which they apply. Thus the words in c. 21. l. c. *occasione laicæ recognitionis* plainly refer to the assisa (recognitio) ultimæ præsentationis, and not, as Bœhmer thinks, to a species of investiture.

(*d*) Bracton, 143.

(*e*) With Bracton, 120 b. 121, *cf.* c. 6. 7. 10. 12. X. de homic. 5. 12 and 2. X. 5. 14.

(*f*) Bracton, 410. 243 b. 396 etc.

(*g*) Br. 185. Eisdem vero modis amoveri possunt a sacramento, quibus etiam testes amoventur a testimonio.

(*h*) Bracton, 427 b.—ut si tenens spoliatus fuerit......et non restitutus in toto vel in parte, non respondebit tenens ante restitutionem, quia *nudi contendere* nec inermes nos inimicis opponere debemus; from c. 3. Caus. IV. qu. 2.

(*i*) Bracton, 302.

(*j*) Bracton, 67: de gradibus successionis et parentelæ.

upon the power of the secular arm, than for a vigorous application of the provisions of the Canon law. Certain it is, that at that flourishing period of its fortunes, the Church endeavored in vain to establish certain rules of the Canon law, to which the legal judgment of the English nation felt a strong instinctive repugnance (*k*). Bracton on his part firmly restricts the papal power within the limits of its peculiar sphere, and defends the rights of the secular power against the encroachments of the Church with a boldness remarkable for that age. He seeks at great length to determine the respective spheres of jurisdiction of the clerical and the secular courts, and his accounts of the relations of the former to the latter are of especial interest. The excesses of authority upon the part of the clerical courts were counteracted by writs of prohibition and by threats of punishment, in spite of the *literæ domini Papæ* (*l*). The opposite views held concerning patronage and special bastardy especially, gave rise to frequent occasions for the use of such means. On the other hand the secular power lent its assistance to the Church for the enforcement of its commands. Thus a person excommunicated for being in contumacy more than forty days, might be placed in custody by the king's command upon the requisition of the clerical judge, in order to compel his obedience to the court Christian (*m*). The peaceful co-operation of the courts of both

Relations between the king's courts and the courts Christian.

(*k*) This is shown especially in the attempts to introduce into England the legitimatio per subsequens matrimonium, and to draw causes relating to advowsons before the clerical courts. The Decretal c. 3. X. de jur. 2. 1 (addressed to the king of England) had no effect. [Upon the dispute concerning special bastardy, *cf.* Chapter XVI.—*Tr.*]

(*l*) Bracton, 250. 251. 401–411. E.g.: Rex talibus judicibus. Ostensum est nobis ex parte A., quod cum in curia nostra......arramavit quandam assisam ......versus B...... Idem B. timens, sibi posse opponi notam bastardiæ......antequam per nos ordinario loci inquisitio de legitimitate probanda......demandata, literas dni. Papæ ad vos directas impetravit, ut de legitimitate sua cognoscatis, ...ut per hoc remaneat hereditas......contra consuetudinem regni nostri,...... et approbatam a sede apostolica:......et cum hoc sit manifeste contra consuetudinem regni......vobis prohibemus ne in causa illa procedatis; 405.

(*m*) Bracton, 427. 408 b. The requisition of the Ordinary ran: Excellent. Dno. suo H. dei gratia, etc......talis N. permissione divina Exon. episc. salutem. ......Serenitati regiæ presentibus intimamus, quod A......propter ipsius contu-

jurisdictions is shown by the writs of consultation mentioned by Bracton (*n*).

---

maciam......excommunicationis vinculo innodatus per XL dies in excomm. perseverans eccles. negligat parere censuræ...... Quia vero regia Majestatis eorum solertiam solet reprimere, qui ecclesiasticis præceptis obedire negligunt...... celsitudinis vestræ brachium invocamus, quod ecclesia minus valet in hac parte, dignetur regia supplere Majestas.

(*n*) Bracton, 302. 307. 406.

CHAPTER VII.

BRACTON'S INFLUENCE IN ENGLAND—EDITIONS.

WE shall conclude this First Part by some remarks upon the importance and value, which have been attributed to Bracton and his work in England. We have no direct proof of the time when the book itself first appeared, but its circulation, some twenty years after its composition, is established by a document of the year 1277, given by Selden, which relates to the loan of a copy of it (*a*). We have, however, the clearest proof of the importance of Bracton's influence in works of other writers written somewhat later.

Circulation of Bracton's work.

Bracton's treatise stands just upon the boundary between two different periods in the history of English law. Before his time the chief sources from which the law was derived, were custom and the authority of usage. Legislation, partially from the sad internal troubles of those times, had hardly any opportunity to interfere in the development of the law. Hence a written exposition of the jus non scriptum was then most opportune. But after Bracton's day a change took place, and under Edward I. legislation became most active, and soon added to the law a rich mass of reforms, changes, and essential innovations. As many of the defects and doubts pointed out by

Its place in English legal history.

(*a*) Selden ad Flet. 2 § 2: Universis præsentes literas inspecturis R. de Scardeburgh, archidiaconus salut. Noveritis me recepisse et habuisse, ex causa commodati, librum quem dominus *Henricus de Breton* (sic!) composuit, a venerabili patre, domino R. dei gratia Bathon. episc., per manum magistri Thomæ Becke, archidiac. Dorset; quem eidem restituere teneor in festo St. Johan. Baptistæ anno dom. MCCLXXVIII. In cujus rei testimonium præsentibus sigillum meum appensum. Datum Doveræ die Veneris post purificat. Virg. glorios. anno MCCLXXVII.

Bracton are removed by the new statutes, it is probable that these reforms were greatly furthered by his work, and that it thus united with the new legal progress and development in stimulating and increasing the scientific study and treatment of the law. The first start in this new legal development may have been given by Edward the First's plan of codifying the whole English law, of which we have an historical account (*b*), while Bracton's labors served as examples inciting to emulation. Bracton's work, indeed, very soon ceased to be entirely equal to the wants of the times; it contained much that had become obsolete, and needed much that was new. While jurists still prized the copiousness and detail of his commentary, those characteristics were rather obstacles to students. The want of a less extensive commentary and one at the same time including the new statute law, seems consequently to have led to the composition of the works we are about to mention. Their more or less direct dependence upon Bracton is a proof of the esteem in which he was held, and of his ever having been considered *the best and truest authority for the Common law.*

Its relation to the subsequent English medieval law books.

The title of the first of these law books, expressly declares it to be an abridgment of Bracton. Its author is Gilbert de Thornton, Chief Justice in the reign of Edward I. It was composed about the year 1292, and bears the following title:

Thornton.

> "Incipit summa de legibus et consuetudinibus Angliæ a magistro *Henrico de Bryctona* composita tempore R. Henrici filii Johannis, quam quidem summam dominus *Gilbertus de Thornton* tunc capitalis justiciarius domini regis in Anglia secundum statuta et leges tunc usitatas ad utilitatem posteriorum diligenti studio postmodum abbreviavit sub compendio, anno regni regis Eduardi filii regis Henrici vicesimo."

(*b*) Selden ad Flet. 2. § 4. gives the following remark of one of the judges from a roll of 35 Henry VI.: le quel roy (Eduard I.) fuit appurpose daver mise tout en certain et en escripture, et commence de ceo faire liver de et par plus sages hommes del ley deins le realme, ses Juges et autres.

Thornton's work is not yet printed. Selden, who had examined a manuscript, has given a full account of it (*c*). From the words, "secundum statuta et leges tunc usitatas," we should expect the new statutes to be taken into consideration, but the author contents himself with omitting what is obsolete in Bracton. The course of Bracton's commentary is followed in general, particularly the division into persons, things and actions, but the external distribution is into eight books, and the law of dower and that of inheritance are postponed to the conclusion. From the retention of some of Bracton's quotations from the Code (*d*), it may be inferred that the rest of his civil law matter is respected.

The next work which we shall consider is one which is in print, and which for that reason alone is of more importance to us. It is that known under the following title: "*Fleta, seu Commentarius Juris Anglicani*" (*e*). Next to Bracton this is the largest of the English medieval law books. Its anonymous author states in his preface (which imitates that of Glanville) that the purpose of his work is to give *brevi volumine* a general view of the law

Fleta.

> "ut non sit necesse quærenti librorum capitulorumque numerositatem evolvere, cum brevitas collecta, quod quærit, offert sine labore."

He has taken Bracton's work as his foundation, or rather has appropriated it to such an extent that the greatest part of Fleta is extracted from Bracton, for the most part with the use of the latter's words, but with the omission of details which do not answer the epitomizer's purpose. The author cuts down the developments and amplifications of the original to what is most necessary, and omits the greater number of the examples, cases, forms etc. Some passages are, however, transferred from Bracton word for word. The abbreviation is, nevertheless, so considerable, that even with the

(*c*) Selden ad Flet. 2. § 4.

(*d*) L. c. 3. §§ 1. 2., mention is made of the citation of C. ad legem milit. (i.e. Juliam) L. omnes = L. 3. C. 9. 27; of C. de donat. ante nupt. L. cum multæ = L. 20. C. 5. 3.

(*e*) Concerning Fleta, v. Reeves, II. 279; Biener, Inq. Proz. 222 *sq.*, Engl. Geschw.-Ger. II. 287.

author's own additions, his work is not half as large as Bracton's. The merit of the author of Fleta lies in his own additions. Putting aside alterations, some of which were necessary and some optional, these additions consist in the insertion of many provisions of the new statutes in their proper places; in completely remodelling, and treating with special detail some subjects which Bracton has only lightly touched upon (*f*) (for which Fleta furnishes illustration and commentary); and finally in adding matter completely new, which is sometimes indeed very loosely connected with an exposition of the law (*g*).

Examining Fleta in its relation to the Roman law, we find no express citations of the text of the Corpus Juris. Some of Bracton's quotations are, however, reproduced with general references, such as ad hoc facit *lex*, *lex imperatoria* (*h*). In one passage, III. 2. § 12. the Institutes are referred to: "secundum quod *Institutis* legitur." The Roman law passages which the author of Fleta extracts from Bracton are almost always repeated word for word, and we meet again, in almost an unaltered form, the matter of the Institutes and of Azo's Summa in the chapters de rerum adquisitionibus, de accessionibus, de actione debiti (obligationibus), de emptionibus, de locato et conducto, de obligatione oriente ex quasi contractu, II. 56–60; III. 1–3. etc. I have found additions of Roman law matter in the chapter de dotis constitutione, V. 23, which are not due to Bracton, but to the author's own knowledge or to some other source. The following Canon law authorities are mentioned: the Decretals c. 2. X. qui filii 4. 17 and c. 2. X. de servis non ordinandis 1. 18 (*i*).

(*f*) Especially so in regard to the procedure in personal actions which Bracton has treated very meagerly.

(*g*) Fleta II. 2–40, gives a view of the organization and jurisdiction of the different courts, and II. 71–88, a dissertation upon matters of rural economy which is most interesting for the history of the manners and customs of the period.

(*h*) Flet. I. 38. § 15. III. 3. § 12: quia omnino hoc prohibetur in *lege*. § 15: verba autem *legis* sunt, etc. III. 10. § 3.

(*i*) I. 14. Et ad hoc facit *decretale* cujus verba sunt hæc: inter A. veterem (must mean virum) et B. etc.; II. 51. § 5, Inhibitum est enim et *in decretalibus* statutum, quod nullus episcopus spurios aut servos, donec a dominis suis fuerint manumissi, ad sacros ordines promovere præsumat.

The system of Fleta agrees only partially with Bracton's. The external division of the work is into six books, which are subdivided into chapters and sections (*j*). The first fifteen chapters of the first book treat of the law of persons; the others discuss criminal actions. The second book is entitled de actionibus personalibus, and includes the heads de testamentis, de emptionibus and de locato, placed by Bracton under modes of acquisition. The third book is entitled de rerum acquisitionibus, and corresponds mainly to Bracton's second. The three last books treat of actions in rem in almost the same order as Bracton, and also discuss the law of inheritance in connection with the writ of right.

Selden's researches have placed it beyond doubt that Fleta was written in the reign of Edward I. (*k*). There are statutes and cases mentioned which serve to fix the date of the work more closely. The statutes of Acton Burnel de mercatoribus (11 Edward I.), of Westminster the second and of Winchester (both 13 Edward I.), and cases of 14, 17 and 18 Edward I. (1286, 1289 and 1290) are mentioned (*l*). From these data Biener thinks that the work was composed shortly after 1290. In one place, however, the submission of Scotland is referred to:

> "II. 13. § 1. Est inter cetera quoddam officium quod dicitur Cancellaria, quod......episcopo debet committi simul cum cura majoris sigilli regni, *cujus substituti sunt omnes cancellarii in Anglia, Hibernia, Wallia et Scotia.*"

This passage and the fact that the recognition of the English supremacy by the Scotch took place during the year 1292 (*m*) compel me to place the composition of Fleta after 1292.

(*j*) According to the preface, the work is divided in tres partes principales: prima de Charta libertatum Angliæ et statutis, secunda de personalibus et tertia de realibus actionibus ordinatur. This division is evidently not that of the work.

(*k*) Selden ad Flet. 10 §§ 1. 2. In consequence of a clearly corrupt passage I. 20. § 59 the book had been asserted previously to belong to the reign of Edward II. and even to that of Edward III.

(*l*) Fleta I. 24. § 3; II. 3. § 9. 10. 12; II. 63. § 7; II. 64.

(*m*) Pauli Gesch. von England, IV. 67 *sq.*

It is well known that this work is not called Fleta from the name of the author, but from that of the Fleet prison, because the preface declares it to be

> "tractatus iste, qui *Fleta* merito appellari poterit, quia in *Fleta de jure Anglorum* fuit compositus."

This is usually connected with the fact that Edward I. in 1289 imprisoned several of his judges for official misconduct. It has been supposed that the author of Fleta was one of these judges, a conjecture which however seems to me improbable (*n*).

Britton.

We come now to the Norman-French tract of *Britton.* The date of this legal treatise is somewhat later than Fleta, being about the year 1297. It does not indeed stand demonstrably in as near connection with Bracton as the previous works. It however shows the authority which was conceded to him, for it is most highly probable that *it bears his name.* According to Selden's conjecture, which is also adopted by Biener, and which is quite probable, the name *Britton* is nothing more than one of the many variations for that of Bracton, while the book itself is a compendium or modification of the older work, to which the name of Bracton himself has been given (*o*). I have not myself had an opportunity of examining Britton, and can therefore give no opinion upon the manner in which the Roman law is made use of, nor of course upon the relation of the

---

(*n*) Selden ad Flet. 10. § 3. and after him Biener Inq. Pr. 223. The reasons upon which my doubts are based are as follows. In the preface the king is praised for his vigorous administration of the laws. The words:

> "et quidquid effrenis audet et immoderata præsumit ambitio suæ potentis auctoritatis censura castigat,"

apply very fitly to the punishment of the judges, but could scarcely come from the mouth of one of the guilty men themselves. The same can be said of the exhortation addressed in the same tone to judges I. 17. Moreover, the passage in the preface upon which the name of Fleta is based, seems hardly to come from the author. From the tenor and contents of the preface and its clear mistake in regard to the division of the work (v. note (*j*) above), it may rather be supposed to be the addition of another hand. This can indeed only be positively settled by a comparison of the manuscripts.

(*o*) Concerning Britton, v. Selden l. c. 2. § 3; Reeves II. 281; Biener Inq. Pr. 224. 225.

work to it. Biener remarks that there is less to be found in it than in its predecessors.

Later estimate of Bracton.

With the beginning of the fourteenth century the period of the legal treatises closes. For the time following until the conclusion of the middle ages, it is necessary, in order to determine Bracton's authority and ascertain his influence upon the development of the common law, to make researches through the extensive collections of cases known as the year books—an investigation presenting much difficulty and few results. Some data have been collected by Biener, to which the reader is referred (*p*). Upon the revival of scientific legal inquiry in England greater attention was, however, paid to Bracton and the older authorities in general. Thus as early as 1534, I find Bracton mentioned twice in company with Glanville in Fitzherbert's New Natura Brevium (*q*). Sir William Staunford makes greater use of him in his Pleas of the Crown, which was written about 1555. But the use which Sir Edward Coke has made of Bracton in his Institutes and especially in the commentary upon Littleton is remarkable. Coke throughout recognizes Bracton not only as an original historical source but also as an authority for existing law, and the rich materials which Bracton affords for investigation are of more importance in his than in any previous researches. At this time Bracton's work appeared in print. The first edition was published in folio in 1569. It was edited anonymously; the preface is signed T. N. The editor remarks that there had long been a great desire for the publication of the work, and that he had compared and used several manuscripts. The second edition, which was published in quarto in London in 1640, is a reprint of the former, in which no alterations have been made, and in which the folios have the same enumera-

Year books.

Coke.

Editions of Bracton's work.

(*p*) Biener, Engl. Geschw.-Ger. II. 294–297. [See Appendix; note to Chapter VII. I have, as yet, been unable to obtain Biener's work on the English Jury. In the hope of doing so before the Appendix is printed, I delay the note here necessary.—*Tr.*]

(*q*) The name of Britton is mentioned f. 17, 189 (edition 1652), but the context shows that it is our author who is referred to.

tion. This latter edition is that which I have used. I cannot agree with Reeves that Bracton's text is in general incorrectly printed, and consequently do not consider a new edition absolutely necessary (1). An historical and explanatory commentary is however desirable.

Modern estimate of Bracton.

Since the seventeenth century there has been but one opinion in England concerning the importance and value of Bracton. Legal historians such as Reeves and Spence, and commentators like Blackstone, Stephens and others, alike esteem him as the leading authority for the older Common law. They regard Bracton's work as the source from which a large number of general legal truths, which are now existing law, derive their origin or their first confirmation. Even at the present day, after a lapse of six hundred years, judges occasionally go back to Bracton, and apply his opinions as existing law (*r*).

(*r*) Spence I. 121 *sq.* [Here also see Appendix; note to Chapter VII.—*Tr.*]

(1) From the *various readings* given at the close of the editor's preface, it may be inferred that all the manuscripts of the work which he had seen contained the interpolated reference, f. 253 b., to the statute 3 Edward I., A.D. 1275 (see ante, Chapter I. note (*f*)). They may all have been copied by ignorant scribes after the author's death from some copy which had never undergone his revision. Such a copy may have been made from the manuscript borrowed from the Bishop of Bath in 1277 (see note (*a*) above). From the *various readings* thus given by the editor, it may also be inferred that he had not seen any manuscript of Bracton which contained the word "*seductionem*" in place of "*seditionem*," f. 118 b., line 7. Mr. Emlyn, a very accurate and learned antiquarian, states in a note to 1 Hale P. C. 77 that "in most of the manuscripts of Bracton the word in this place is '*seductionem.*'" Hence it may be inferred that "most of the manuscripts" were not seen by the editor of the printed work. Selden in the Dissertatio ad Fletam, II. § 4, mentions the manuscripts of Bracton as numerous, and as differing from one another in some particulars not noted in the printed edition, which are not without bibliographical interest. There thus are doubtless manuscripts of Bracton which his editor never saw. Whether the text of any of them is purer than that from which the work has been printed is a question which cannot be answered except in England. Upon the answer, it may be decided whether a new edition is needed. There are eight manuscripts of Bracton mentioned in the Record Commission's Catalogue of Harleian manuscripts, and four in the Appendix to the Report of the Record Commission (1837). If the best manuscripts were collated by the editor of the work now in print, the present edition is quite as good as any new one which would probably be producible, and perhaps much better. The numerous errors and obscurities are doubtless not Bracton's, but those of transcribers.—*Tr.*

Bracton has ceased to be a stranger in Germany since writers like Biener, Gneist, and others have included the English law and its history within the range of their researches. The position which he holds in relation to the Roman law, which is the special subject of our attention, must alone make him esteemed in Germany. During the middle ages Bracton was the first to discuss the Roman law in connection and amalgamation with the local domestic law (*s*). A place must therefore be assigned him in the history of the Roman law.

His place in the history of the Roman law.

(*s*) The *Siete Partidas* of Alphonso X. were first completed about 1265.

PART SECOND.

DETAILED INVESTIGATION OF THE ROMAN LAW IN BRACTON'S WORK.

PART SECOND.

DETAILED INVESTIGATION OF THE ROMAN LAW IN BRACTON'S WORK.

CHAPTER VIII.

INTRODUCTORY.

HAVING treated generally of Bracton and his relation to the Roman law, I now enter upon the second part of my task, that of investigating *in detail* the Roman elements and rules of law, which our author has adopted and digested in his work. We shall thus get a complete picture of the extent to which the Roman law then obtained in England, and clearly ascertain what was its influence upon the English law. With the exception of some deviations made for the sake of convenience I have entirely followed the order of Bracton's work (*cf.* Chapter II.) in this investigation, and have had sometimes occasion to refer also to Glanville and Fleta. I shall premise a few remarks upon the notions of law, right, etc. with which Bracton introduces his system. These are to be found in chapters 4 and 5 of the first book, entitled "*de justitia et jure*" and "*qualiter dividitur jus,*" and comprehend the same subjects as those discussed in the first two titles of Justinian's Institutes. We find there the familiar definition of justice:

Subject of the Second Part.

General legal notions.

Justitia.

> "est autem justitia constans et perpetua voluntas jus suum cuique tribuens,"

in connection with Azo's distinction between divine justice, *justitia in creatore*, and human justice, *justitia in creatura*. The different meanings of *jus*, *jurisprudentia*, and *æquitas* are then given; æquitas being defined as:

Jus.

Æquitas.

> "rerum convenientia, quæ in paribus causis paria desiderat jura, et omnia bene coæquiparat" (*a*).

These are followed by the well-known *tria præcepta juris*, and by the division of law into *jus publicum* and *jus privatum* (*b*). *Jus privatum* is divided into *jus naturale, jus gentium* and *jus civile* (*c*). *Jus civile*, called with special reference to England *jus consuetudinarium* or *jus commune*, according to Bracton is based upon *lex* and *consuetudo*. *Lex* is explained, according to L. 1. D. de leg. 1. 3., as:

Jus publicum, jus privatum.

Jus civile.

Lex.

> "commune præceptum, virorum prudentum consultum,......rei publicæ sponsio communis;"

Consuetudo.

of *consuetudo* he says that it

> "quandoque pro lege observatur......et vicem legis obtinet; longævi enim temporis usus et consuetudinis non est vilis auctoritas,"

(from L. 2. C. quæ sit long. 8. 53) (*d*).

(*a*) Bracton, 2 b. 3. Azo in Inst. I. 1. f. 240. [In regard to æquitas *cf.* also the passages f. 12 b.; de *æquitate* tamen per officiorum Justiciariorum tenebitur donator, etc.; f. 23 b.: æquitas tamen sibi locum vendicat in hac parte, quod dominus non sit in damno, etc. Of the exercise of Equitable jurisdiction by a separate council or tribunal we find no trace in Bracton. This does not, however, prove that in his day the royal council may not have given relief in some of the cases, in which it afterwards heard complaints and referred the petitioners to the Chancellor for that redress which the ordinary tribunals could not afford.—*Tr.*]

(*b*) Bracton, 3 b. Jus publicum is there quod ad statum *rei publicæ* pertinet; in Azo, ad statum *rei Romanæ*.

(*c*) Bracton, 3 b. 4. The passage: "jus gentium,......quod a naturali jure *procedit*, eo quod jus naturale omnibus animalibus commune," must be corrupt; instead of *procedit*, *recedit* should be read as in L. 1. § 4. D. de jur. 1. 1. So also in Azo 240 b.—"quod a naturali *recedere* facile intelligere licet."

(*d*) Bracton, 2.

CHAPTER IX.

THE LAW OF PERSONS.

IN chapters 6–11 of his first book Bracton treats of *Persons*, a subject which constitutes the first part of his tripartite system. We must not, however, expect a complete commentary upon the law of persons, like that in the corresponding titles of the Institutes I. 3–13. Our author, on the contrary, confines himself to general observations upon the relations of personal status (*a*).

Law of Persons.

Bracton begins by giving the Roman *summa divisio* personarum,

Servi, villains.

"quod omnes homines sunt aut liberi aut servi."

Villains (nativi, villani) are without hesitation legally assimilated to the Roman servi. So too he says of them

"servi aut nascuntur, aut fiunt" (*b*).

But the rule:

"partus sequitur ventrem,"

which obtained in the Roman law, was in England modified by marriage.

That rule held good if the issue was born out of marriage, but did not do so in the opposite case: the child born in wedlock followed the father, and was bond or free according as the latter was bond or free, even if the mother was of a different status. Here, however, the rule of favorable interpretation, laid down in pr. J. de ing. 1. 4, was recognized (*c*).—The power of the lord over the bondsman, the *potestas dominica*, is seen in the rule:

Potestas dominica.

(*a*) Fleta's system is more consistent, the subjects relating to the law of persons being placed together in the first book.

(*b*) Bracton, 4 b. Fleta, I. 1. 2. 3. § 1 = Azo, f. 241. No. 1–3.

(*c*) Bracton, 5. (Fleta I. 3. 4.): Liber vero et ingenuus dici poterit, qui statim ut natus est liber est, sive ex duobus liberis......sive ex duobus libertinis......

"quidquid per servum adquiritur, id domino adquiritur;"

and the question regarding acquisition by a *servus communis* is decided by Bracton, if not in the words, at least in the sense of the Roman jurists, f. 25 b.:

"item esto, quod plures sint domini, et servus sit communis, si contrahat et stipuletur, quæro, cui istorum dominorum, utrum uni vel ambobus? Respondeo: Si uni tantum, ipse totum habeat, si ambobus, tunc commune erit secundum quod servus fuerit stipulatus. Sed semper ratio habenda est de parte dominorum;"

(evidently from § 3. Inst. de stipul. serv. 3. 17.). The condition midway between bond and free occupied by libertini was a consequence of manumission, upon the form and effects of which Bracton is, however, silent. Like the Roman law, Bracton recognizes a freedom in fact, arising from the lord's neglect to enforce his rights, which protected the villain's possession of liberty (*possessio, seisina libertatis*), and burdened the lord with the proof of servitude in the quæstio de statu. Such apparently free persons were called *statu liberi*, a Roman name borrowed from an entirely different legal relation. Conversely, those in an apparent condition of bondage are styled by Bracton *statu servi* (*d*).

Libertini.

Statu liberi.

Statu servi.

In connection with bondage, the *patria potestas* is mentioned by Bracton as another relation of power founded upon the distinction between *homines sui juris* and *alieno jure subjecti*. It was not, however, the Roman in-

Patria potestas.

sive nascatur ex matre ancilla et patre libero, dum tamen extra villenagium et *in libero thoro*, dum tamen *ex matrimonio*. Item ex matre libera et servo extra matrimonium. Et sufficit matrem esse liberam vel tempore illo quo concepit, vel tempore quo parit, vel saltem in medio illorum temporum, licet ancilla facta fuerit, quia non debet calamitas matris ei nocere, qui in utero est. = pr. J. 1. 4. Littleton was aware of this disagreement between the Roman and the English law; he says, § 187: Mes si niefe (nativa) prend frank home a son baron, lour issue est franke. Et c'est *contrarie a la ley civille*, car la est dit: partus sequitur ventrem. *Cf.* also Fortescue p. 42. No notice appears to have been taken of c. un. X. de nat. ex lib. ventr. 4. 10. [*Cf.* Hallam, Middle Ages II. 171, 172, text and notes, (Ed. Boston, 1853); on "*extra villenagium*," see Reeves I. 269 note (*a*).—*Tr.*]

(*d*) Bracton, 7. 7 b. 190 b. 194, 197. [See Reeves I. 270. Concerning statuliberi, v. D. de statuliberis 40. 7.—*Tr.*]

stitution of that name which he had in view, for he mentions none of its characteristic peculiarities and effects, except the general principle borrowed from § 3. J. de pat. pot. 1. 9. that

> "qui ex te et uxore tua nascitur, in tua potestate est, item qui ex filio tuo et ejus uxore nascitur,......qui vero ex filia tua nascitur in potestate tua non est, sed in patris ejus vel avi, vel proavi" (*e*),

and the rule, which he afterwards discusses more fully:

> "pater est quem nuptiæ demonstrant."

Emancipatio.

Familiar grounds for dissolving the patria potestas are mentioned, viz., mors naturalis et civilis, dignitas episcopalis, and *emancipatio*, the last referring to the forisfamiliation of children at that period common in England:

> "si quis filium suum *forisfamiliaverit* cum aliqua parte hereditatis suæ" (*f*) ([1]).

Adoptions were not in use in England, and Bracton is consequently silent concerning them (*g*).

Sex, sanity.

Some principles of Roman law also occur in the distinctions which Bracton makes in regard to sex and sanity. Thus we find the provision of the Roman law in regard to hermaphrodites:

> "*hermaphroditus* comparatur masculo tantum vel feminæ tantum secundum prævalescentiam sexus incalescentis" (*h*),

and L. 14. D. de stat. hom. 1. 5. concerning monsters:

> "—item qui contra formam humani generis converso

(*e*) Bracton, 6.

(*f*) Bracton, 6 b: item morte civile, ut si pater damnetur propter *aliquam feloniam* commissam (Azo, 242 b.: "si damnetur in *metallum vel opus metalli vel deportetur in insulam*")......vel perpetuo exuletur, si autem relegetur ad tempus nihilominus retinebit liberos in potestate sua.

(*g*) I have found adoptions mentioned in one passage only (f. 63 b.), but in an entirely different sense: Legitimantur (liberi) quandoque quasi *per adoptionem*, ...ut si uxor de alio conceperit, quam de viro suo,......si vir ipsum in domo suo susceperit et......nutriverit in filium, etc. Adoption here must mean the recognition of issue born in matrimony.

(*h*) Bracton, 5. Fleta, I. 5. § 3.

([1]) *Cf.* Reeves, I. 42, 110.—*Tr.*

> more procreantur...... Partus autem qui membrorum officia ampliavit, ut si sex digitos habeat,......talis inter liberos connumerabitur" (*i*).

The distinction which Bracton makes between furiosi, non compotes mentis, as completely incapable of acting (except in lucid intervals) and fatui, stulti, ideotæ, also recalls Roman authorities (*j*).

(*i*) Bracton, 5. Fleta, I. 5. §§ 1. 2.

(*j*) Bracton, 12. 15. 375 b. 420 b. Flet. I. 11. § 10.

CHAPTER X.

THE LAW OF THINGS.

Introduction.

Bracton follows his Roman models in his commentary upon the general doctrines relating to things, and rights concerning them. He does so especially in regard to the division of things, and the terminology of the Corpus Juris which he has adopted in his chapter de divisione rerum has since remained fixed in the English law. Thus we find it said there (as in Azo in Inst. 2. 1.):

Law of things.

Division of things.

> "rerum quædam sunt in patrimonio nostro, et quædam extra...... Quædam vero nec sunt in patrimonio, nec extra, sicut jura" (*a*)—

and also:

> "aliæ *corporales*......, quæ tangi possunt, sicut terra, fundus,......aliæ *incorporales*......,sicut sunt jura, quæ videri non possunt nec tangi" (*b*).

We find also the tertia divisio rerum, under which are distinguished *res communes* (aer, aqua profluens, mare, litus maris), *res publicæ* (flumina, portus, usus riparum), *res universitatis* and *res nullius*. Under the last are enumerated *res sacræ* (which with Bracton include *res religiosæ*) and *res sanctæ* (*c*).

Before going further in the discussion of the law of things some general remarks are here necessary.

(*a*) Bracton, 7 b. Flet. III. 1. § 1–3. Azo, 243 b. No. 7.

(*b*) Bracton, 7 b. 10 b. = Azo, 246 b. No. 8.

(*c*) Bracton, 7 b. 8. Azo, 243 b. 244. Bracton, 14 b. 44 b. 170 b. 180 b. where res sacræ and res religiosæ are throughout promiscuously used.

Comparison of the English and Roman systems as to the law of things.

It is well known that the distinction between realty and personalty running through the English law, has corresponding to it two distinct systems of law, one comprehending the law of immovables and the other that of movables. These two legal systems divide not merely the law of things, but also the law of obligations, of inheritance and of procedure. Although this distinction is not theoretically laid down by Bracton, we can see that it was already in existence, and can recognize how it affected the way in which the influence of the Roman law operated. Now, while the principles of the Corpus Juris were adopted without hesitation for movable property by Bracton and the English lawyers of his time (*d*), the progress of the Roman law towards influencing the law of immovables was checked by the powerful obstacle of a legal system, already fully developed and complete within itself, which had grown up on purely feudal foundations, and which was thoroughly penetrated with the spirit of the feudal polity. Some particulars were indeed borrowed from the Roman law, but its fundamental principles were unaffected by any contact with the Roman law and its influence. Hence arose the difference existing between the Roman and the English laws even in their fundamental notions of the right of property and of rights or interests in things. The principle of the English law that there could be no allodium except in the king's hands, and that the possession of all land was subject to some sort of feudal dependency (*e*), was alone irreconcilable with the Roman notion of dominium, which was most clearly defined, and which was to a certain extent constructed upon an ideally complete model of ownership. Furthermore, the Roman *Real rights* or interests, issuing in certain defined cases out of the dominium, were founded upon the greater or less degree of legal power and control over the thing

(*d*) *Cf.* Chapters V. and XII.

(*e*) Coke, 1 Institutes 1 b., expresses the principle thus: "prædium domini regis est directum dominium, cujus nullus est autor nisi deus ipse."

itself in which the particular interest existed (1), and therefore rested upon an ultimate basis purely *legal*. But the different kinds of feudal dependency to which land might be subjected and the duration and strength of the possession, were the causes which created the English system of interests in the possession or seisin of land (2). These latter hence rested upon an ultimate basis of *facts*, presented by the actual characteristics and peculiarities of the feudal system, to which the law was compelled to adapt itself. The interests so created were thus rights whose character must be termed *relative*, when compared with the *absoluteness* of that of the Roman Jura in re (*f*). This relative character is equally seen in the highest possible of these rights, the *feodum* (v. note (*f*)), although Bracton does not hesitate to identify it with dominium and

---

(*f*) The following summary will serve to give an insight into the legal system in force in Bracton's time. All land being subject to the feudal tie, the land was styled *tenementum*, the possessor *tenens*, and the lord *dominus*. Bracton himself does not give any technical expression for this dependent relation, but at a later period that of *tenure* was adopted. According to the character of this feudal relation the following distinctions were made: I. Lay holdings, comprising the following: 1. *Feuda militaria*, quæ tenentur per homagium et servitium militare; 2. *Socagia libera;* 3. *Villenagia;* II. Ecclesiastical and eleemosynary holdings in libera eleemosyna (frankalmoign). This division applied only to the *manner* of possession; the *interests* in the possession of land were classified according to the duration of their existence. These were as follows: I. *Tenementa libera* (*franktenement, freehold*, in later language), comprising interests for periods not definitely ascertained. They were, 1. The greatest possible interest, feodum (fee simple), or possession with unlimited inheritance, i.e. quod quis tenet ex quacunque causa sibi et heredibus suis, Bracton, 263 b. He who held quoad feodum was seised in dominico suo ut de feodo, Bracton, 372 b. 2. *Possession for a term of life, ad terminum vitæ*, e.g. the widow in her dower, or the widower *per legem Angliæ.* These life interests are not to be considered as usufruct, but rather as revocable property. II. Interests less than liberum tenementum, comprising: 1. *Possession for a time definitely fixed, ad tempus, ad terminum annorum, firma* (whence firmarius), even when it exceeded any possible limit of a man's life. To the firmarius Bracton ascribes usus and ususfructus in contradistinction to proprietas and feodum. 2. Mere *precarious* possession, *ad voluntatem.* Bracton, 27, 39 b. [As to an interest depending upon the life of another, *cf.* Bracton, 26 b.—*Tr.*]

---

(1) The dominium, or right of property, being the exclusive and unlimited power and control of a person over a thing. *Cf.* Savigny, Traité de Droit Romain, trad. Guenoux I. § LVI, p. 362.—*Tr.*

(2) *Cf.* 2 Blackstone's Com. 104–106. Spence I. 33, 34.—*Tr.*

proprietas. But it would be an error to look upon the true owner according to our notions as always having the *feodum;* for the feodum of one man as of possessory right might co-exist with the jus majus or better right of another. The latter being mere right (*merum jus*) without any corresponding possession, is of no importance for the law of things (3)(*g*). —In this case as in others the Roman terminology failed to describe legal relations, which were foreign to the Roman law. Hence when Bracton occasionally uses such expressions as "ususfructus, fructus, usus, habitatio," he does not at all connect with them the legal notions which the Corpus Juris has made current with us. On the contrary those words are used by him *in a general meaning and not in a technical sense,* and without reference to any particular legal institution of the Roman law. It would thus be a great error to confound the ususfructus ascribed to a firmarius (v. note (*f*)) with the usufruct of the Roman law, or even to apply to it any particular principle of the Roman institution (*h*).

Influence of the Roman law upon the English doctrine of possession.

Notwithstanding, however, the obstacles which the English law of realty opposed to the progress of the Roman law, the latter exercised an important influence upon a subject relating both to the law of immovables and that of movables, viz., the doctrine of *possession.* The clear distinction between proprietary right carrying with it possession (and thus constituting legal possession) and actual corporal possession, is found in the English as well as in the Roman law. It might indeed be difficult to prove that the theory of possession in England, or rather the appearance of possession as a peculiar institution of the English law, was connected with the introduction of the Roman law. There can, however, be no doubt of the Roman character of the doctrine of possession in Bracton and Fleta (*i*), which must not only be regarded

(*g*) Bracton, 434 b.

(*h*) Bracton, 207, 220, 259.

(*i*) As early as Glanville, we find laid down the distinction between petitory actions, quæ super proprietate proditæ sunt, and possessory actions, quæ super possessione loquuntur; I. 3. XIII. 1. 9.

(3) I.e. has no place in a classification of interests in things according to their quantity.—*Tr.*

as existing law in their day, but must also be considered as the basis of subsequent legal development upon this head. Their doctrine of possession is based and developed upon Roman notions and ideas, and those writers look at the subject in the same light as the contemporary Civilian school, and in many respects copy its views (*j*).

Upon this subject, which will be discussed in the next Chapter, Bracton shows a more than ordinary freedom in the use of his authorities, and, in his mode of exposition especially, has not followed Azo so closely as elsewhere.

(*j*) Bruns in his Recht des Besitzes im Mittelalter (Law of Possession in the Middle Ages), § 42, has indeed mentioned the Norman law, but appears not to have made use of Bracton.

CHAPTER XI.

POSSESSION.*

Bracton has not assigned a special place in his system to the doctrine of possession, but it is discussed incidentally to the acquisition of property and in connection with traditio, in chapters 17–22 of his second book. There is also much relating to it to be found scattered through the work, especially in the tract *de assisa novæ disseisinæ* (*a*).

Possession in Bracton.

The notion of *possessio, seisina*—for both words are promiscuously used—is defined and explained in Azo's words as follows:

Its definition.

> "possessio est corporalis rei detentio, *corporis et animi, cum adminiculo juris* concurrente...... Et possessio ideo dicitur *rei detentio*, quia naturaliter tenetur ab eo, qui ei insistit scilicet *corporaliter*" (*b*);

and Azo's conception of *Civil* and *Natural* possession, which was at that time most generally diffused, is thus reproduced by Bracton:

Natural and Civil possession.

> "possessionum autem alia *civilis*, alia *naturalis*. Civilis autem est, quæ *animo tantum retinetur*, naturalis quæ *corpore*."

Natural possession was the pure corporal detention as in Azo, who describes it as that

> "quam quis corpore suo vel oculis et animi affectu adipiscitur;"

Civil possession was the *fiction of possession* which still continued after the loss or cessation of natural possession.

---

* Upon possessory actions v. Chapter XX.

(*a*) Possession is also discussed in Fleta, III. c. 15., de traditionibus et usucapionibus.

(*b*) Bracton, 38 b. Azo in Cod. (7. 32.) f. 189 b. No. 8.

Azo remarks:

> "illam tamen naturalem, *quam retineo animo* firmiter, dico, posse dici, et vere dicitur, *civilis*" (*c*).

Bracton however seems to reject Azo's conclusion that both cannot be united in the same person.

> "Non videtur," says Azo, "quod eodem tempore quis possideat civiliter et naturaliter;"

but Bracton on the contrary adds to the definition, mentioned above, the remark:

> "et potest quis *utroque modo possidere*, scilicet animo et corpore,"

and moreover holds that he,

> "qui ex aliqua justa causa adquisitionis naturalem possessionem habuerit et civilem,"

lost both by a traditio:

> "statim amittit et desinit habere *utramque ex ipsa traditione*" (*d*).

Bracton's view appears in the clearest way in the case of ejection (disseisin). The ejected man lost at first *only* the natural possession and not the civil, because

> "*animo retinere* potest, licet fuerit extra possessionem."

He recovered the former if he succeeded in repossessing himself *recenter incontinenti.* If he made no attempt to do so, or the attempt to redress himself failed, he lost also the civil possession:

> "provideant igitur sibi,......quod injuriam disseisinæ per patientiam, dissimulationem, negligentiam, desperationem, vel negligentem impetrationem non tepescant, per quod amittunt *utramque* possessionem *naturalem scilicet et civilem*" (*e*).

The doctrine laid down of f. 51 that after a person had voluntarily gone away from his land, he still retained the civil and natural possession

> "quousque alius ingrediatur contra voluntatem suam,"

appears to be derived from a foreign source, but not from

(*c*) Bracton, 38 b. 41 b. Azo, loc. cit. No. 9.

(*d*) Bracton, 51.

(*e*) Bracton, 41 b. 51. 163. 163 b. 164. 164 b.

Azo. The doctrine that

> "*solo corpore,......sine animo* ut post mortem alicujus, donec corpus efferatur ad sepulturam"

possession could be retained,

> "quia ante non erit possessio vacua,"

appears to be original with Bracton, who however does not deduce any practical consequences from it (*f*).

The expression of the Roman sources "in possessione esse" is found in Bracton denoting natural possession, and the axiom:

> "longe aliud est *possidere* (*seisitus esse*) quam *esse in possessione* (*in seisina*),"

expresses with him the opposition between mere possession in fact and possession judicially cognizable. In this sense natural possession is ascribed to all "qui alieno nomine possident," such as villains, guardians, procuratores, usufructuarii and firmarii. Hence was derived the principle

> "ille possidet cujus nomine possidetur" (*g*).

The person "cujus nomine possidetur" had in these cases the civil possession; and adds Bracton

> "per tales sibi retinet naturalem,"

whereby he evidently would express the same idea which Azo, f. 190 b., clothes in these words:

> "cum igitur per me habeat naturalem (possessionem), ergo ipsam habeo per eum" (*h*).

Other analytical divisions of possession then adopted by jurists are reproduced by Bracton. Of these I will only briefly mention the distinction between possessio *justa* and *injusta* (*i*), depending solely upon the jus possidendi; that between possessio *vera* and *imaginaria* (fictitia, colorata), a distinction occurring in the Roman cases,

Other analytical divisions of possession.

(*f*) Bracton, 41 b. 262.

(*g*) Bracton, 165, 167 b. 168. 206. Fleta, IV. 3. § 1.

(*h*) Bracton, 165, 167 b. 168. 206.

(*i*) Bracton, 39. 51. 195 b. Item quis rem alienam potest juste possidere...... et injuste, sed tamen secundum diversos respectus; juste quantum ad feoffatorum suum et alios omnes, qui jus non habent; injuste tantum quantum ad ipsum qui jus habet scilicet verum dominum.

> "ubi quis se gesserit ac si possideret, cum alius possideat;" and where one "dolo desiit possidere" (*j*);

and lastly the distinction between *possessio rei corporalis* and *possessio juris vel quasi-possessio*, depending upon the nature of the object possessed (*k*).—The subject of quasi-possession will be discussed in another part of this chapter.

Acquisition of possession.

Civil law principles also obtain in the *acquisition of possession.* At the very beginning of this subject we find the rule:

> "adquirere nemo potest possessionem nisi *utroque modo corpore et animo*,—neque animo per se, neque corpore per se" (*l*).

Animus possidendi.

The first of these two elements, viz. the intention of possessing, is called *animus possidendi et retinendi*, voluntas retinendi possessionem, affectus possidendi (*m*), and presupposed capacity to will. Hence the following persons were incapable of acquiring possession: servi, ab hostibus capti, quia ab aliis possidentur, and furiosi:

> "tales enim cum animum non habuerint adquirendi, in tali statu adquirere non possunt seisinam" (*n*)

(*cf.* L. 1. § 3. D. de adquir. et amitt. poss. 41. 2.).

Corpus.

The nature of the other factor in acquiring possession, the *corpus*, can be ascertained from what is laid down in relation to occupatio and traditio. In regard to occupatio, it is here only necessary to refer to the next chapter, where it is discussed, and where we shall find merely the Roman principles of *apprehensio.* Traditio, which Bracton treats of incidentally to donatio, demands however a closer examination in this connection.

(*j*) Bracton 39. 183. 269 b. 432 b.: item alienare poterit sine dolo post impetrationem et post summonitionem,......quod de summonitione nihil sciverit. ......Si autem fecerit contrarium,......haberi debet pro possessore,......ut de term. S. Mich. anno reg. H. 4, incipiente 5. [*Cf.* L. 25–27. D. 6. de rei vind. 1.—*Tr*]

(*k*) Bracton, 38 b. De re autem corporali ideo dicitur, quia incorporalia non possunt possideri, nec usucapi, nec sine corpore tradi, quia per se traditionem non patiuntur. Ideo dicuntur *quasi possideri*, tradi enim possunt vel quasi, per patientiam et usum.

(*l*) Bracton, 38 b. 41 b. 51 etc.

(*m*) Bracton, 39. 39 b. 40. 41 b.

(*n*) Bracton, 44 b. 375 b. 420 b.

Traditio.

Traditio ([1]), says Bracton, in uno sensu (i.e. as a mode of acquiring possession):

"nihil aliud est, nisi in possessionem inductio de re corporali."

Possession was thereby obtained only

"tunc, quum donator corpore et animo recesserit a possessione sine aliqua spe et animo revertendi ut dominus, et cum donatorius *in possessione vacua extiterit corpore et animo et cum voluntate retinendi possessionem;* ......quia donator nunquam desinit possidere, donec donatorius plenarie fuerit in seisina, nec jacebit seisina aliquo tempore medio vacua" (*o*).

Possessio vacua.

From this and a series of other passages, it appears that Bracton lays the principal stress upon the existence of a *possessio vacua* as a requisite of the traditio, a view which we know controlled the contemporary Civilian doctrine upon the subject, in consequence of an erroneous generalisation of certain passages of the Corpus Juris, (L. 2. § 1. D. de act. emt. 19. 1; L. 13. C. de distr. pign. 8. 28; L. 12. C. de prob. 4. 19.) (*p*). With detailed and even casuistical accuracy, he determines whether a possessio vacua should or should not be considered as existing in particular cases, (especially considering whether the old possessor or his representative had remained on the land in company with the new possessor); in doubtful cases he discriminates whether the traditio was vera or imaginaria according to the ascertainable purpose of the man making it (*q*). The possession is expressly declared not to have been vacua:

"si quis in eadem possessione fuerit, sicut procurator,

(*o*) Bracton, 39 b. 41 b. Fleta, III. 15. § 10. 11.

(*p*) So also in Azo ad Inst. 2. 1. f. 246. No. 4.: item si emptor inducatur in *vacuam possessionem*. *Cf.* Fleta III. 15 § 11.

(*q*) Bracton, 41 b.–43. 49–51. The case in which the former possessor returned is mentioned as doubtful.

([1]) As the word *traditio* in Bracton applies to movables or personalty as well as to land (e.g. f. 40: si quis equum emerit in ipsa traditione suus erit), it therefore may be translated either *delivery* or *livery*, according to its application to the one or the other.—*Tr.*

> colonus, inquilinus, servus vel amicus,......cum non sit in seisina nomine donatorii" (*r*).

It was necessary that this evacuation or act whereby possession was given up by one party should, in order to complete the traditio, be succeeded by the immediate assumption and retention of actual possession by the other (*s*), (which retention, however, it seems was only required to be temporary). The practical details of the traditio also show the adoption of Roman principles. Thus Bracton says f. 40:

Different forms of traditio.

> "non necesse est, omnes glebas circumire, nec ubique nec undique pedem ponere; fieri debet traditio per ostium et per haspam vel annulum, et sic erit in possessione de toto ex voluntate et aspectu et possidendi affectu" (*t*) (evidently after L. 3. § 1. D. de poss. 41. 2.).

Thus too the so-called symbolical traditio is recognized as admissible, f. 44:

> "item si claves cellulæ vivariæ vel horreorum tradiderit quis domino vel procuratori, vina et merces tradi videntur" (after L. 1. § 21. D. de poss. 41. 2.).

So also, on f. 41, he says:

> "idem etiam dici poterit et *assignari*, quando res vendita est in conspectu quam venditor dicit se tradere, ut si ducatur in horreum vel campum" (*u*).

Bracton is likewise familiar with the so-called brevi manu traditio, f. 41:

> "si tibi vendam quod tibi accommodavi (sic) aut apud te deposui,......et sic mutaverim causam possessionis, hoc fieri poterit sine mutatione possessionis. Ex hoc

---

(*r*) Bracton, 42 b.

(*s*) Br. 43: item incipit quis possidere quando de voluntate donatoris nactus fuerit possessionem vacuam, corpore et animo retinendi; and 41 b.: cum ingressus fuerit vacuam possessionem per se vel per suos.—Fleta III. 15. § 10.

(*t*) Bracton, 40. 42 b.: quia licet totum fundum non circumierit, vel in omni parte non extiterit, tamen ex ipsa traditione totum adquisivit, cum tempore traditionis eo animo seisinam nactus est, quod totum fundum cum pertinentiis possideat usque ad terminos. Fleta III. 15. § 6. The traditio per ostium, etc., mentioned in the text refers to the symbols of delivery usual in England as early as the Saxon period.

(*u*) *Assignari* is taken from Azo 246. No. 4.: assignari, quum res vendita vel donata est in conspectu, quam venditor vel donator dicit se tradere. [The above is the so-called longa manu traditio.—*Tr.*]

enim quod patior, rem meam esse tuam ex aliqua causa vel apud te esse, videor tradere" (*v*) (from L. 9. § 5. D. de adqu. rer. dom. 41. 1.).

Acquisition of possession by representatives.

The acquisition of possession by means of representatives must have been of much practical importance in Bracton's time, judging from the extent of his remarks thereupon, part of which are taken verbatim from L. 1. § 2 *sq*. D. de poss. 41. 2. These representatives might be either free and independent persons, or those "quos sub potestate nostra habemus" (children, servi). The former might be either voluntarily constituted (procuratores), or imposed (curatores, custodes). As in the new Roman law, in the case of free representation ([2]) it was of no importance that the principal should have a special knowledge of the acquisition:

> "adquiritur nobis possessio per procuratorem et tutorem etiam *nobis ignorantibus*. Et si dicatur per eos nobis non adquiri, qui nostro nomine accipiunt, futurum est, ut nec ipse possideat scil. procurator vel tutor, cui res aliena sic tradita est, nec is, qui tradidit, quia concessit possessionem" (= L. 1. § 20 D. de poss. 41. 2.).

But it was requisite that the representative should have capacity to will:

> "quia si minorem vel furiosum, liberum vel servum, miseris ut possideas, nequaquam per eos videris possessionem apprehendisse, quia intellectum non habent" (= L. 1. § 10. loc. cit.) (*w*).

(*v*) Bracton, 40. Item sufficit pro traditione corporali nuda voluntas domini ad alium, quasi mutata causa possessionis;......ut si quis rem alicui locaverit vel concesserit ad terminum vitæ vel annorum et postea eidem vendiderit vel donaverit, licet eam ex tali causa primo non habuerit, tamen eo quod ipse dominus patitur, eam ex tali causa......apud eum esse, sua efficitur.

(*w*) Br. 43 b. 44. Per communem servum adquirimus etiam singuli in solidum, si ad hoc tamen agat servus, ut uni tantum adquiret; si autem ad hoc non agat, tunc singulis adquiritur in communi (= L. 1. § 7. D. de poss.)...... Item per servum, qui in fuga est, dum tamen a nullo possidetur, quia quamdiu ab alio non possidetur, a domino videtur possideri (= § 14. l. c.). Fleta III. 15. § 14.

([2]) Upon free and necessary or non-free representation, v. Savigny, Traité de Droit Romain, trad. Guenoux, III. § 113, especially note (g).—*Tr.*

The acquisition of possession was therefore effected thus: corpore, i.e. corpore alieno in the person of the representative, and animo, viz., by the intention, which the latter must have, of obtaining possession for his principal (*x*). In one passage I find the *constitutum possessorium* mentioned as a substitute for the traditio:

> "f. 41, item illud idem poterit assignari, cum rem illam, quam tibi donavi et non tradidi, conducam a te, et sic videor tradere."

(Verbatim from Azo f. 246 n. 4., where L. 77. D. de rei vind. 6. 1. is cited.)

Except some remarks specially referring to ejection (disseisin), we find few general principles in Bracton concerning the *loss of possession*. It has already been shown in speaking of civil and natural possession, how Bracton considers that one might continue even after the other had ceased. Consistently with this view the *utrumque in contrarium actum* of the Roman rule in L. 8. D. de poss. 41. 2., is indicated as being necessary to the removal of *both* elements of possession, and the following rule is laid down and frequently repeated in various forms of the same purport:

Loss of possession.

> "amitti non poterit *sine utroque* scilicet animo et corpore, quia retinetur animo sine corpore et corpore sine animo, et cum utrumque defecerit, amittitur ex toto" (*y*).

In accordance therewith, a person not having the capacity to will could not lose a once acquired possession, and he who had abandoned his land under pressure of poverty still retained possession *animo civiliter* (*z*).

(*x*) This appears from the expressions used in many places: nomine suo (i.e. domini) corpore alieno;—nomine suo. Br. 41. 41 b. Hence if any one had assumed possession as negotiorum gestor only and the dominus did not ratify, the gestor acquired no possession, quia nomine suo non accepit, sed alieno. Br. 42 b. Fleta III. 15. § 13.

(*y*) Bracton, 39. 41 b. 45 b. 51 *et al.;* also Fleta III. 15. § 2.

(*z*) Bracton, 165 b.:—quia in ipso furore animum mutare non poterit, nec desinere possidere, quia consentire non potest, nec dissentire. *Cf.* 375 b. 420 b. —Bracton, 262.: item si per paupertatem possessionem dereliquerit, ita quod dominus capitalis pro defectu servitii tenementum in manum suam ceperit,...... vel alio excolendum dederit,......satis moritur tenens seisitus, quia *animo retinet civiliter*, licet corporaliter non fuerit in possessione: evidently after L. 4. C. de poss. 7. 32.

Quasi-possession.

To the foregoing view of the possession of things, some remarks upon *juris quasi possessio* should be added. Bracton, indeed, lays down no general principle upon quasi-possession, but it is evident from his treatment of its application to particular matters that, without altogether sharing the extreme views of the contemporary Canonists, he takes a position nearer theirs than that of the Glossators, who confined themselves on this subject to the platform of the Roman Law (*aa*). According to Bracton, quasi-possession existed in the cases of servitutes (which were only predial, personal servitutes being altogether unknown to the English law), granted franchises and privileges (tolls, markets, jurisdictions, etc. called *libertates*), and rights of presentation (*bb*). Whether the jus advocationis itself was the object of quasi-possession or was included in the corporal possession of the land to which it was appurtenant, is left in doubt by Bracton (*cc*).

Acquisition and loss of quasi-possession.

Bracton's views concerning the acquisition and the loss of quasi-possession are obscure, and it may be presumed that the doctrine upon this subject was not fully settled in his time. In regard to servitutes and libertates, it was *not* in general necessary that there should be an actual *usus* of the right in order to acquire possession; it sufficed

> "quod quis habeat *aspectum* et *possidendi affectum*."
>
> "Adquiruntur scilicet ex solo aspectu accipientis...... et possidendi voluntate et affectu...... Et sic adquiritur possessio servitutis *ante usum*."
>
> "Hujusmodi libertates, cum a rege concessæ fuerint, statim......quasi possidentur" (*dd*).

(*aa*) *Cf.* Bruns, Recht des Besitzes (Law of Possession) 185 *sq.*

(*bb*) Bracton, 52 b. 53.: hujusmodi jura (servitutes) quasi possidentur ex fictione juris. Among servitutes the communia pasturæ occupies a most prominent place; 221 *sq.* Upon libertates, v. Bracton, 55 b.–58.; seisina præsentandi, 53 b. [*Cf.* also Reeves I. 306.—*Tr.*]

(*cc*) Bracton, 53 b.:—quia sine corpore (ad quod pertinet) recte possideri non possit, licet ab aliquibus dicatur, quod *quasi* ad similitudinem servitutis. [*Cf.* in Reeves I. 352, 353.—*Tr.*]

(*dd*) Bracton, 40. 53. 56. 222: et quo casu statim erit in seisina, licet statim

The usus however served to prove the continued existence of the possession: *possessio retinetur per usum* (*ee*). It is true that in one passage a usus permitted by the owner of the servient land is spoken of as being necessary, in order that possession might be acquired, but from the expressions, "*pacifice sine interruptione*, per longum tempus," this would appear to refer to the duration of possession required in cases of usucapio (*ff*). The seisina præsentandi however could only be acquired through at least *one* actual exercise of the right, and he only had seisin who himself had exercised the right at the *last* vacancy, or whose ancestor had done so (*gg*). The possession of a servitus (and also that of a franchise) was lost by *non usus* (longa patientia, negligentia), and also by dispossession, i.e. hindrance of the usus (*hh*).

Grades of possession.

In conclusion it will be interesting to see how Bracton regards the relation which possession bears to the right of property and the different possessory interests. Discriminating between the element of fact and the element of law existing in possession, he makes a scale arranged according to the different proportions in which those elements might be combined, which must include all posses-

---

non immittat averia sua (pecora). Bracton, 226 b. The two agencies, corpus and animus, are distinguished in the following passage: et semper videtur uti voluntate et animo civiliter, et præsentia et aspectu naturaliter; Bracton, 225.

(*ee*) Bracton, 53. 56. [See Reeves I. 306.—*Tr.*]

(*ff*) Bracton, 52 b.: patientia trahitur ad consensum, et adquiritur possessio juris per usum, ut si dominus proprietatis......ex patientia permiserit uti vicinum suum, præsens et sciens, in fundo suo aliqua servitute,......sicut in pastu pecorum, itinere vel actu,......*per longum tempus pacifice sine interruptione.* [See Chapter XV.—*Tr.*]

(*gg*) Bracton, 53 b. 240 b.: cum autem semel præsentaverint et ita sunt in *seisina præsentandi.*—Hoc est quod *ultimo* præsentaverit aliquem, qui ad præsentationem suam admissus fuerit et institutus. *Cf.* Glanville IV. 1.; XIII. 20; Fleta V. 11 *sq.* Hence the possessory action was called assisa ultimæ præsentationis. This seisina præsentandi gave rise to the Decretal of Alexander III. c. 19. X. de jur. patr. 3. 38.:—"si tempore præsentationis suæ ille, qui eum præsentavit, *jus patronatus ecclesiæ possidebat......* Si vero non possidebat, sed tantum credebatur patronus esse, cum non esset, nec *possessionem patronatus* haberet (hence distinguished from the possessio juris patronatus) *secundum consuetudinem Anglicanam*, poterit" etc.

(*hh*) Bracton, 53. 56. 222. 225. 232.

sory relations from the highest to the lowest presented by the different English interests in realty.

The gradation is as follows: 1. possessio quæ *minimum* habet *possessionis* et omnino *nihil juris*, neque aliquam juris *scintillam*, nuda pedis positio, i.e. the possession of him who without right intruded upon an hereditas jacens or other possessio vacua; 2. Possession with *parum possessionis et nihil juris:* i.e. violenta, clandestina, precaria possessio; 3. Possession with *aliquid possessionis sed nihil juris:* the possession of a guardian, firmarius, tenant for years etc.; 4. Possession with *multum possessionis et nihil juris*, i.e. that of a freehold for life; 5. Possession with *plus possessionis et multum juris:* the fee to a man and his heirs; 6. Lastly, he had *plurimum possessionis et plurimum juris*, who united in himself the liberum tenementum, feodum et proprietatem (jus merum), i.e. could show not only the jus possessionis but also the jus proprietatis, the *conjunctio seisinæ cum jure.* This double right, *jus duplicatum*, was called *dreit dreit* (*droit droit*) in the legal language of the period (*ii*) ([3]).

(*ii*) Bracton, 39. 160. 206 b. 372 b. Fleta III. 15. In an entirely different sense Azo makes the following distinction, f. 190: possessio quæ *multum juris* habet......; alia possessio quæ *plurimum* habet *facti* in adquirendo et *parum juris* in retinendo. Bracton's terminology however seems to be borrowed from this passage. [The spelling adopted by Bracton, f. 206 b., is *dreit dreit.—Tr.*]

([3]) *Cf.* Reeves, I. 319, whose view is as follows: "Of land a man might have either what they called *possession*, or what they called *jus*, or *proprietas*. Possession was of various sorts, and divided by very nice distinctions. One was said to be *quædam nuda pedum positio*, which they called *intrusion;* and this contained in it, says Bracton, *minimum possessionis*, and *nihil juris*, being somewhat of the nature of a disseisin: in both it was a *nuda possessio*, till it received a *vestimentum* by length of time. Another was a precarious and clandestine possession, attended with violence, which acquired no *vestimentum* by length of time; and this, says the same authority, had *parum possessionis*, and *nihil juris*. A possession for term of years, as it gave nothing but the usufruct, was considered in a degree higher, as having *aliquid possessionis*, but *nihil juris*. The next was for life, as dower, or the like; and this being a step higher, was said to be *multum possessionis*, but still *nihil juris*. The next degree was, where a person had the freehold and fee to him and his heirs; and then he was said to have *plus possessionis*, et *multum juris:* and he who had the freehold, fee, and property, united in himself, had *plurimum possessionis*, and *plurimum juris*, which was called *droit droit*, and contained the highest degree of property and possession; except that, even then, some other person might have *jus majus*, or greater right."—*Translator.*

CHAPTER XII.

ACQUISITION OF PROPERTY—OCCUPATIO, ACCESSIO, SPECIFICATIO.

BRACTON, as we have already seen from the sketch of his system given in Chapter II., refers the acquisition of property partly to the jus naturale (jus gentium), and partly to the jus civile, although he does not draw any practical conclusions from the distinction. It has also been remarked that when our author treats of the modes of acquisition which belong to the first category, he almost always copies both the matter and form of his Roman authorities (the Institutes, Lib. II. tit. 1. de divisione rerum and Azo's commentary), and even expressly refers the reader to those sources as being, as it were, the ratio naturalis of the law upon such matters (*a*). These principles of the Roman law, as found in Bracton and repeated in Fleta, in fact, at once became common law in England, and are still of practical validity at the present day (*b*). It is true, as we learn from Bracton himself, that a limitation of this proposition occurs where the Common law had framed provisions of its own relating to these modes of acquiring property, or where a particular custom had sanctioned something different. In such cases the Roman law naturally was not applied. This force of the Roman law as a *subsidiary* rule is indicated by Bracton's additions of remarks like the following:

Acquisition of property.

Modes of acquisition by the jus naturale (jus gentium).

> "hæc vera sunt, nisi *consuetudo* se habeat in contrarium,"
>
> "nisi aliquando *de consuetudine in quibusdam* partibus aliud fiat."

(*a*) Bracton, 10.: ut in Institutis plenius inveniri poterit et in Summa Azonis.

(*b*) Fleta, III. 2. *Cf.* Stephen, Commentaries, II. 5, 16 *sq.*

Parallel passages from Bracton and Azo upon occupatio, accessio, specificatio.

Without going into details, it is, I think, only necessary to give the following extracts from Bracton and Azo side by side, which the reader can compare.

BRACTON Lib. II. c. 1. § 2.

Jure autem gentium *sive naturali* dominia rerum adquiruntur multis modis. Inprimis *per occupationem* eorum, quæ non sunt in bonis alicujus *et quæ nunc sunt ipsius regis de jure civili et non communia ut olim* (*c*), sicut sunt feræ bestiæ, volucres et pisces, et omnia animalia quæ in terra et in mari et in cœlo et in aere nascuntur, *ubicunque capiantur;* et cum capta fuerint, incipiunt esse mea, quia mea custodia coercentur; et eadem ratione si evaserint custodiam meam et si in naturalem libertatem se receperint, desinunt esse mea et rursus fiunt occupantis. Recipiunt autem naturalem libertatem tum, cum vel oculos effugerint in aere libero, et *non sub captura mea,* vel ita sunt in conspectu meo, ut impossibilis sit eorum persecutio (*d*).

§ 3.

Item continet occupatio *piscationem, venationem et apprehensionem.* Et nec sola persecutio facit rem esse meam. Nam etsi feram bestiam ita vulneraverim,

AZO in Inst. II. 1. f. 244. No. 7 sq.

Jure autem gentium dominia adquiruntur nobis multis modis, ut ecce in primis *per occupationem* eorum, quæ non sunt in bonis alicujus, ut sunt feræ bestiæ, et volucres et pisces et omnia animalia, quæ in terra, mari et cœlo i.e. in aere nascuntur, *sive capiat quis in suo sive in alieno; dominus tamen fundi prohibere poterit ingredientem venandi aut occupandi gratia* etc......,et qua ratione captum incipit esse meum, quod mea custodia coercetur, eadem ratione, nisi evaserit custodiam meam et in naturalem libertatem se receperit, desinit esse meum et rursus fit occupantis. Recipit autem naturalem libertatem, quum vel oculos meos effugerit in aere libero *non sub cappa mea,* vel ita sit in conspectu, ut difficilis i.e. impossibilis sit ejus persequutio.

Continet igitur occupatio *piscationem et venationem et apprehensionem.* Sola enim persequutio non facit rem esse meam. Nam etsi feram bestiam ita vul-

(*c*) This remark of Bracton's is not entirely correct, as not all but only *certain* res nullius, such as thesauri, certain fish (balena, sturgio) and wreckum maris, belonged to the king.

(*d*) *Cf.* Fleta III. 2. § 1.

BRACTON.

ut capi possit, non tamen est mea, nisi eam cepero, immo erit potius occupantis, quia multa accidere solent, ne capiam. Item si in laqueum, quem venandi causa tetendi, aper incidit *cum coertione* (!), eum exemptum abstuli, erit meus, si in potestatem meam pervenerit, *nisi consuetudo vel privilegium se habeat in contrarium* (*e*)......

AZO.

neraverim, ut capi possit, non tamen est mea, nisi cepero, immo erit *posterius* occupantis, quia multa accidere solent, ne capiam. Et hoc est adeo verum, ut si in laqueum, quem venandi causa *posueram*, aper incidit et, *quum cohæret*, exemptum eum abstuli, fit meus, si in potestatem meam pervenerit. *Consuetudo tamen generalis in eo repugnat......*

§ 4.

BRACTON.

Hæc, quæ dicta sunt, locum habent in animalibus, quæ *omni tempore* fera permanserunt. Si autem animalia fera facta fuerint mansueta et ex consuetudine eunt et redeunt, volant et revolant, ut sunt cervi, cygni, pavones et columbæ, alia regula comprobata est, ut eousque nostra intelligantur, quamdiu habuerint animum revertendi. Nam si revertendi animum habere desierint, nostra desinunt esse...... In domesticis vero tertia regula comprobata est, quod licet conspectum meum effugerint anseres mansueti et gallinæ, quocunque tamen loco sunt, mei intelliguntur esse, et furtum facit qui ea animo lucrandi retinuerit ...... Item locum habet eadem species occupationis in iis, quæ communia sunt, sicut in mari et litore maris, in lapillis et gemmis et ceteris in litore maris inventis.

AZO.

Hæc, quæ dicta sunt, locum habent in animalibus quæ natura sunt fera. Si autem animalia fera facta fuerint mansueta et ex consuetudine eunt et redeunt, volant et revolant, ut sunt cervi, pavones et columbæ, alia regula comprobata est, ut eousque nostra intelliguntur, donec habent animum revertendi. Nam si animum revertendi desierunt, nostra desinunt esse. Revertendi autem animum videntur desinere habere, quum revertendi consuetudinem deseruerunt...... In domesticis enim etc. (as in Bracton).

(*e*) Fleta III. 2. § 2. only says generally:—nam etsi feram bestiam ita vulneraverim, ut capi possit, non tamen est mea, nisi ipsam ceperim, sed occupantis. *Cf.* § 13. J. 2. 1.

BRACTON.

Idem etiam in insulis in mari natis......et in rebus pro derelicto habitis, *nisi consuetudo se habeat in contrarium propter fisci privilegium* (*f*).

AZO.

BRACTON.

Lib. II. c. 2. § 1.

Adquiruntur etiam jure gentium rerum dominia per *accessionem discretam vel secretam, concretam seu continuam;* et quæ ex animalibus dominio tuo subjectis nata sunt, tibi adquiruntur. Item quod per *alluvionem* agro tuo flumen adjecit, jure gentium tibi adquiritur. Est autem alluvio latens incrementum, et per alluvionem adjici dicitur, quod ita paullatim adjicitur, quod intelligere non possis, quo momento temporis id adjiciatur. Nam et si tota die infigas intuitum tuum, imbecillitas visus tam subtilia incrementa perpendere non potest, ut videri poterit in cucurbita et similibus. Si autem non sit latens incrementum immo apparens, contrarium erit; ut ecce vis fluminis partem aliquem ex tuo prædio detraxit et vicini prædio appulit, certum est, tuam permanere, et si longiori tempore fundo vicini

AZO.

l. c. f. 244 b. No 10 sq.

Jure gentium adquiritur etiam dominium *per accessionem, discretam vel secretam, concretam sive continuam.* Nam quæ ex animalibus dominio tuo subjectis nata sunt, tibi adquiruntur. Præterea quod per *alluvionem* agro tuo flumen adjecit, jure gentium tibi adquiritur. Est autem alluvio incrementum latens. Per alluvionem adjici videtur, quod ita paullatim adjicitur, ut intelligere non possis, quantum quoquo momento temporis adjiciatur. Nam etsi tota die figas intuitum, imbecillitas visus tam subtilia incrementa perpendere non potest, ut in cucurbita et similibus...... Si autem non sit latens incrementum etc. (as in Bracton, to the words "Dabitur tamen"). *Utilis tamen rei vendicatio datur priori domino secundum Martinum. Sed dicimus nos dari actionem in factum ut in specificatis duobus.*

(*f*) *Cf.* Bracton, 120.: Wreckum dici poterit quasi derelictum, ut si quid (navis levandæ causa) a nave projectum fuerit ab aliquo sine animo repetendi vel retinendi, id proprie dici poterit wreckum, cum res projecta habita sit pro derelicta. This view consequently does not agree with L. 9. § 8. D. 41. 1. and L. 21. §§ 1. 2. D. 41. 2. [But *cf.* L. 43. § 11. D. de furtis 47. 2.—Things found at sea at so great a distance from land that it could not be shown within what sovereign's dominions they would have come to shore, belonged to the finder, according to Bracton 120, 120 b. The Roman law thus applied, for there could be no consuetudo to the contrary.—And see Bracton, 8. 41 b.—*Tr.*]

BRACTON.

adhæserit et arbores, quas secum traxerit, radices in eum fundum egerint, ex eo tempore videntur fundo vicini adquisitæ. *Dabitur tamen priori domino utilis vendicatio secundum quosdam. Sed cessat rei vendicatio*, quia alterius facta est crusta, et alia dicenda est arbor aliæ terræ alimento (*g*).

AZO.

Cessat autem rei vendicatio, quia alterius est facta crusta, et alia dicenda est arbor aliæ terræ alimento.

§ 3 (*h*).

Hæc de accessione, quæ fit tantum divina natura operante; est et alia, quæ fit tantum natura humana operante, quæ fit per *adjunctionem* unius speciei ad alteram ejusdem generis vel diversi per *applumbaturam vel ferriliminationem*, secundum quod infra legitur, et ibi dicitur, quæ pars alteri debet accrescere (*i*). *Si autem per applumbaturam, minor cedit majori vel preciosiori, sed si neutra preciosior, quilibet suum vendicabit.*

No. 14.

Hæc de accessione, quæ fit divina natura tantum operante. Superest, ut videamus et de accessione, quæ fit humana natura tantum operante; hoc autem fit per adjunctionem, *quæ adjunctio fit per applumbaturam aut per ferruminationem.* Fit autem applumbatura, *cum aliquo mediante diversa corpora ejusdem vel non ejusdem speciei jungantur, plumbo sive aliquo simili......*

Si quidem per applumbaturam, ut puta, minor cedit majori, vel si nulla sit major, cedat altera alteri preciosiori, vel si neutra sit preciosior, neutra cedat alteri......

§ 4.

Vendicabit etiam sibi locum jus accessionis in ædificiis per hu-

Vendicat sibi etiam locum jus accessionis in ædificiis per hu-

(*g*) In Fleta III. 2. § 6. the passage runs thus: *opinio quorundam* tamen est, quod utilis rei vendicatio in persona prioris domini observatur, quorundam vero, quod cessat rei vendicatio quia alterius facta etc. In my opinion the "quidam" can only mean *English* lawyers, so that we have here a direct proof of the application of the Roman law in foro.

(*h*) In § 2, the insula in flumine is discussed.

(*i*) The "infra" refers to the subsequent citation of the Institutes. *Cf.* Fleta III. 2. § 12.: secundum quod Institutis legitur, ubi dicitur quæ pars alteri etc.

BRACTON.	AZO.
manæ naturæ laborem, ut si quis in solo suo alienam materiam ædificavit, ipse dominus intelligitur ædificii, *quia omne, quod inædeficatur, solo cedit. Nec tamen is, qui materiæ dominus fuerat, dominus esse desinit, nec suum potest eximere, sed pro eo duplum consequetur, et si dirutum sit ædificium, quod suum fuerat, vendicare poterit, nisi fuerit duplum consecutus* (*j*). E contrario si quis de suo in alieno solo ædificaverit mala fide, materiam præsumitur donasse, *si autem bona fide, solvat dominus soli precium materiæ et mercedem fabricatorem. Hoc, quod prædictum est, locum habet si ædificium sit immobile.* Si autem mobile, aliud erit, ut ecce horreum frumentarium novum ex tabulis ligneis factum in prædio Sempronii positum, non erit Sempronii.	manæ naturæ laborem. Ecce enim cum in suo solo quis alienam materiam ædificaverit, ipse dominus intelligitur ædificii, *quia omne, quod inædificatur, solo cedit. Nec tamen, is qui materiæ dominus fuerat, dominus esse desinit, sed tantisper; neque vendicare potest eam, neque de ea re ad exhibendum agere per legem XII tabul., qua cavetur*, ne quis tignum alienum ædibus suis injunctum eximere cogatur; sed duplum præstet pro eo per *actionem*, quæ dicitur *de tigno injuncto. Si autem aliqua causa diruptum sit ædificium, poterit materiæ dominus eam vendicare, si non fuerit duplum consequutus.* Et ex contrario, qui ædificat in alieno solo de sua materia, si quidem mala fide, præsumitur donasse. Si vero bona fide, *habet doli exceptionem, ne aliter teneatur restituere, nisi dominus soli pretium materiæ solvat et mercedes fabrorum.* Ubi autem quod ædificatur mobile est, ut ecce horreum frumentarium novum ex tabulis ligneis factum in prædio Seji positum, non erit Seji......
§ 6 (*k*).	f. 245 b. No. 4.
Alia autem accessio erit divina natura et humana co-operante, et quæritur ex ea dominium; ut ecce Titius alienam plantam in	Fit etiam accessio divina natura et humana co-operante, et quæritur ex ea dominium. Ut ecce Titius alienam plantam in

(*j*) Fleta, III. 2. § 12., does not speak of the action for the duplum, but only says: modicum pretium consequetur. [The text of Fleta appears to me to be obscure and corrupt.—*Tr.*]

(*k*) § 5, which is omitted, treats of pictura, scriptura etc.

BRACTON.

solo suo posuit, ipsius erit planta; et ex diverso, si Titius suam plantam in *Menii* solo posuerat, Menii erit planta, si modo utroque casu radices egerit, unde versus:

Quidquid plantatur, seritur vel inædificatur,
Omne solo cedit, radices si tamen egit.

Sed antequam radices egerit, permanet ejus cujus prius fuerat; *et hoc est adeo verum, ut si vicini arbor ita terram Titii oppresserit, ut in ejus fundo radices egerit, Titii erit arbor. Ratio enim non permittit, ut alterius sit quam ejus in cujus fundo radices egerit. Item si in confinio arbor posita sit et in vicini fundo radices egerit, communis erit, nec licebit vicino radices excidere. Et hoc verum est, si arbor mea in vicini fundo radices egerit, sine quibus vivere non possit, quod communis esse debeat; si autem satis vivere possit sine radicibus illis, non erit communis.* Qua autem ratione plantæ solo cedunt, quum radices egerint, et ædificia immobilia, eadem ratione cedunt frumenta, quum sata fuerint, et solo coaluerint, sive fortuito casu cecederint in terram sive non.

AZO.

suo solo posuit, ipsius erit planta; et ex diverso si Titius suam plantam in *Mevii* solo posuerit, Mevii planta erit, si modo utroque casu radices egerit. Ante autem quam radices egerit, ejus permanet cujus et fuerat. *Et est hoc adeo verum, ut si vicini arbor ita terram Titii presserit, ut in ejus fundo radices egerit, Titii effici arborem dicimus; rationem etiam non permittere, ut alterius arbores eæ intelliguntur, cujus in fundo radices egissent.*

Et item prope confinium arbor posita, si etiam in fundo vicini radices egerit, communis fit; non tamen licet eas recidere, nisi forte præmissa denunciatione......

Vel distingue: in radicibus sint tales, sine quibus non poterat vivere, an poterat; in primo casu arbor sit communis, in secundo non, sed agi possit, jus non esse ita radices immissas habere. Qua autem ratione plantæ, quæ terra coalescunt, solo cedunt, eadem ratione frumenta quoque, quæ sata sunt, solo cedere intelliguntur...... Quod autem dixi in satis et plantatis, dicerem, etsi sola divina natura plantæ vel frumenta solo coaluerunt, ut si fortuito casu ceciderunt in terram......

Lib. II. c. 3. § 1.

Adquiritur et nobis res per *specificationem*, ut si quis de aliena materia speciem fecerit ali-

l. c. No. 5 sq.

Adquiritur etiam dominium *per specificationem;* qui enim speciem aliquam de aliena ma-

BRACTON.	AZO.
quam, dominus erit speciei, qui fecit.	teria facit, dominus est speciei, si bona fide id fecit, non si mala fide. (Here follows a fuller explanation of Specification.)
§ 2.	
Est et alius modus adquirendi per *confusionem*. Confunduntur itaque liquida ut mel et vinum. Confunduntur etiam solida licet cum difficultate magna, ut species, sicut aurum, argentum, plumbum et ferrum, et quod ex iis redigitur erit commune (sive separari possit sive non) inter eos, de quorum voluntatibus corpora sive species confunduntur. Si autem casu fortuito fiat confusio et separari non possunt, idem erit. Si autem separari possunt materiæ, unusquisque partem ponderis et mensuræ habebit, quam habuit in rudi materia (*l*). Si autem frumentum alicujus mixtum fuerit cum frumento alterius, non erit frumentum inter eos commune; sed quilibet de acervo suo vendicabit partem pro modo sui frumenti. Nec fieri poterit communicatio frumenti, quia singula corpora manent in sua substantia (*m*).—	Est alius modus adquirendi dominium, ut *per confusionem*. Confunduntur autem liquida, ut mel et vinum; item species, ut argentum et aurum, plumbum et ferrum. Si igitur materiæ aliquorum his volentibus confundantur, corpus, quod ex his redigitur, erit commune, possint vel non possint separari; quod si casu fortuito fiat confusio, idem est, si tamen separari non possint...... Ubi autem voluntate dominorum mixtæ sunt species, ut frumentum, fit communicatio, aliter non; sed siquis de acervo pro modo sui frumenti vendicabit partem, et arbitrio judicis continetur, ut is eximet quale cujusque fuerit frumentum. Non fit tamen communicatio frumenti, quia singula corpora manent in sua substantia.—

(*l*) Fleta III. 2. §§ 14–16.

(*m*) Bracton mentions here the thesauri inventio. As by the English law treasure-trove belonged to the king, he could not adopt the Roman theory of acquiring treasure. He however explains thesaurus in the words of L. 31. § 1. D. 41. 1., when speaking of the crime of occultatio thesauri on f. 120:

> "est autem thesaurus quædam vetus depositio pecuniæ vel alterius metalli, cujus non exstat modo memoria, ut jam dominum non habeat."

CHAPTER XIII.

DONATIO.

Modes of acquisition by the Civil or Municipal law.

Donatio in the English law.

BRACTON proceeds to speak of the modes of acquisition by the Civil or Municipal law in chapter 4. of his second book. Of these donatio occupies the first place. He designates it as "magna celebris et famosa causa adquisitionis." Donatio, however, in its then English sense does not correspond to our Donation. It signified, at least with reference to immovables, *every alienation or gift according to the forms of the feudal system without reference to its distinctive legal effect.* Under this general idea there was therefore included not only the conveyance of a fee (*cf.* note (*f*), Chapter X.) but also that of lesser interests. The application of the word *donatio* in this sense is etymologically due to the stereotype expressions of ancient use in charters, "dedi, concessi, donavi," and is explained by the circumstance that, ***as grants of feuds derived their essential character mainly from the relation of mutual faith between lord and vassal, they were looked upon as acts of*** PURE LIBERALITY ***and the services to be rendered by the tenant were regarded, not in the light of an equivalent, but as effects of that faith, or as modifications defining the nature of the gift itself*** (¹). It is therefore very evident that an English lawyer, when the Roman law came to be better known, could without fear transfer individual principles of the Roman donation to the different English legal relation of the same

(¹) Oportet......quod pecunia vel servitium non interveniat, ne cadat (i.e. donatio) in causam emptionis et venditionis, quia ubi pecunia intervenerit ibi erit emptio, si autem servitium, ibi erit servitii remuneratio; Bracton 14 b. The value and importance of the above remark in the text are such that I have placed it in italics. And see Reeves I. 294 in fin.—*Tr.*

name. This can indeed be seen in the conformity of Bracton's definition to the Roman law:

> "est autem donatio quædam institutio, quæ ex mera liberalitate et voluntate, nullo jure cogente, procedit, ut rem transferat ad alium."

It is also evident in the divisions which Bracton borrows from the same source, viz., that into donatio *inter vivos* and donatio *mortis causa*, and that into *donatio simplex*,

> "ubi in nullo casu donator velit ad se reverti, quod dedit,"

and *donatio conditionalis vel sub modo:*

> "si quis ea mente dederit, ut tunc demum fiat accipientis, cum aliquid fuerit subsecutum" (*a*).

Prohibition of donationes inter conjuges.

More important and more remarkable, however, is the adoption of the Roman prohibition concerning donations between spouses. Bracton lays down as law upon this head:

> "item non valent donationes factæ inter virum et uxorem, non enim vir poterit donare uxori, nec e converso constante matrimonio" (*b*).

The following will explain this peculiar phenomenon. Under the denomination of dower (dos) the English law accorded to the wife after the death of her husband one-third of his lands and tenements for her lifetime; but only so much and no more, even when he had expressly given a larger dower at the time of the marriage. This last provision was evidently established in the interest of the feudal heir (*c*). Such restraint was however easily avoided by husbands by means of donationes durante matrimonio, which, it appears, were originally entirely allowable. The abuse of these latter must however have occurred or been felt shortly *after* Glanville's time, since, while we meet with no trace of a prohibition of donationes inter conjuges in his book, we

---

(*a*) Bracton 11. Fleta III. 3. § 1. = L. 1. D. de donat. 39. 5.

(*b*) Bracton 12 b. 29. Fleta III. 3. § 12 *sq.*

(*c*) Glanville VI. 1.: si vero dotem nominat et *plus tertia parte,* dos ipsa in tanta quantitate stare non poterit; amensurabitur enim usque ad tertiam partem.

find that they are held to be invalid in a case of 8 Henry III. (1224), and that the same doctrine is adhered to in later cases (*d*). As there is no doubt that this legal principle does not owe its existence to the Common law, we can only suppose that, when the want of some provision to supply the defect of the national customary law was manifested, the judges' familiarity with the Roman law led them at once to have recourse to the Roman prohibition concerning donations between spouses in order to justify a prohibition of donationes in the English sense (i.e. gifts between the living). That even at a later period the foreign law was looked upon as the real source of this prohibition is shown by Fleta, who gives the Roman law as authority for it:

"quia hoc prohibetur in lege" (i.e. jure Romano) (*e*).

The extent to which the prohibition was applied, included also such antenuptial donationes as were made "ob causam et affectionem matrimonii," and such donationes as were made to an extranea persona in order to elude its operation (*f*). On the other hand donationes "post divortium factæ" were held valid; and the prohibition was not considered to apply to the so-called *dotis constitutio*, since that was identified with the Roman donatio propter nuptias (Bracton citing in this connection L. 20. C. de don. ante nup. 5. 3.) (*g*).

Dotis constitutio.

Donationes "post factam feloniam" were held to be null by the English law, and Bracton points out expressly the agreement of this principle with L. 15. D. de don. 39. 5.; it must not however be concluded that it was derived from the Roman law, for it should undoubt-

Donationes post factam feloniam.

(*d*) Bracton 29. Et quod hujusmodi donationes non valent, probatur......de term. S. H. anno regni regis H. 8. Com. Notting. de Rob. de Wallingham et Johanna uxore ejus, ubi dicitur, quod non valet talis donatio. Other cases of 15, 17, Henr. III. ibid.

(*e*) Fleta III. 3. § 12. [*Cf.* L. 3. § 10.; L. 9. § 2.; L. 10.; L. 32. pr. *sq.*; L. 33. § 2. D. 24. 1.; L. 10. C. 5. 16.—*Tr.*]

(*f*) Bracton 29.

(*g*) Bracton 29 b. cites a part of the lex: "si igitur......nomine et substantia nihil distat a dote donatio ante nuptias facta viro, quare non ea simili modo et contracto matrimonio dabitur? Sancimus igitur" etc.

edly be connected with the feudal escheat (forisfactura, escaeta) (*h*).

Requisites of the English Donatio.

But, on the other hand, in the requisites of the English donatio we meet with many Roman principles. For its validity it was above all required that there should be free will on the part of the donator and mutual consent on the part of both contractors:

> "— non valet donatio, nisi tam dantis quam accipientis concurrat mutuus consensus et voluntas, scilicet quod *donator* habeat *animum donandi et donatorius animum recipiendi*" (*i*).

Vis.

The requisite free will might be destroyed by the existence of violence or compulsion. The expression *vis* with Bracton includes both. Like Paulus, L. 2. D. quod met. 4. 2., Bracton describes vis as

> "majoris rei impetus cui resisti non potest;"

and according to the doctrine of the contemporary school of civilians he divides it into *vis expulsiva*, *vis compulsiva* "quæ aliquando metum inducit," and other less important kinds, such as vis perturbativa, inquietativa, ablativa etc.

Metus.

Metus is however more closely defined in Azo's words and in the sense of LL. 5. 6. 9. D. l. c.:

> "metus est autem præsentis vel futuri periculi causa mentis trepidatio; et præsentem accipere debemus metum non suspicionem inferendi ejus, vel cujuslibet vani et meticulosi hominis, sed talem, qui cadere possit in virum constantem" (*j*).

It was indifferent whether the compulsion was directly brought to bear upon the individual himself or upon his relatives or dependents, and this principle, which is clearly taken from the Roman law, is expressly shown to be recognized by English judicial authority (*k*).

(*h*) Bracton 12 b. 30 b.—convenit *lex cum consuetudine Anglicana*, F. de don. L. post contr ubi dicitur quod post contractum capitale crimen, *donationes factæ valent*, *nisi* condemnatio subsecuta sit. Selden ad Fletam c. III. 1. has remarked the difference between this reading and our text.

(*i*) Bracton 15 b. Fleta III. 7. § 3.

(*j*) Bracton 16 b. 17. 162. Fleta III. 7. § 1. Azo in Cod. 2. 20. f. 26 b.

(*k*) Bracton 16 b.

As vis or metus destroyed free will, so error prevented consent. Here also our author gives Roman law. He distinguishes between error *in persona*, *in re*, *in numero* and *quantitate*, and *in causa*. *Error in re* was always hurtful:

Error.

Error in re.

> "quia, si donator senserit de una re et donatorius de alia, non valet donatio propter dissensum."

In the case of *error in numero vel quantitate* consent could exist, at least in minus (*l*):

Error in numero vel quantitate.

> "ut si quis decem dederit, et alius senserit de viginti, non valet quamvis major numerus in se contineat minorem, quia uterque in certum numerum non consentit...... Sed si aliquis dederit decem et donatorius consenserit in quinque, valet donatio, quia ambo consentiunt in minorem numerum."

From a misapprehension of L. 36. D. de adq. rer. dom. 41. 1. Bracton seems to have held *error circa causam* to have been unimportant generally:

Error circa causam.

> "si in corpus, quod traditur, sit consensus, non nocet, quamvis circa causam dandi atque recipiendi sit dissentio, ut si pecuniam numeratam tibi tradam, et tu eam quasi traditam accipias, constat ad te proprietatem transire" (*m*).

The delivery of the res donata was essentially necessary to the validity of the donatio, whereby it became *perfecta* and did not remain merely *nuda permissio*. Glanville, indeed, shows that this was the old law in England:

Traditio.

> "quia id intelligitur, secundum *consuetam regni interpretationem*, potius esse nuda promissio quam aliqua vera promissio vel donatio" (*n*);

(*l*) Bracton 15 b. 16.

(*m*) Bracton 16. [See Pothier h. t. Num. LVIII, text and notes. We should here recall the remark in Chapter V. pp. 59, 60, that errors in the statement of Roman law are not to be imputed to ignorance on the part of Bracton. Bracton here states the English law as it was and is (except as in rare instances it might possibly be modified by a court of Equity). He here appears to state the English law as it was, without relying upon the Roman texts.—*Tr.*]

(*n*) Glanville, VII. 1.

and Bracton links the principle that

"non valet donatio, nisi subsequatur traditio,"

partly to the Roman maxim that

"traditionibus et usucaptionibus rerum dominia transferuntur,"

and partly to the theory of *pacta nuda* belonging to the old English law:

"item oportet, quod donationem sequatur rei traditio, ...alioquin dicetur talis donatio potius nuda promissio, quam donatio, et ex *nuda promissione non nascitur actio, non magis quam ex nudo pacto*" (*o*).

Feudal investiture.

This traditio has frequently been compared and made parallel with the investiture of a feud, especially by English jurists ([2]). But in fact it approaches much nearer to the Roman traditio, from which it has certainly borrowed the greater part of its rules. The essential part of the investiture was the creation and symbolical attestation of the relation of faith between the feudal lord and vassal, with which the corporal delivery of the feud or land, which might follow, had nothing in common (*p*). But we see nothing whatever of such characteristics in the English traditio; on the contrary, the English law prescribed for such purposes the solemn performance of homage (*q*), and considered the only purpose of the traditio to be corporal induction into possession.

Now traditio in this sense (*r*) was according to Bracton:

"de re corporali propria vel aliena, de persona in

(*o*) Bracton 16. 39 b. 15 b. Nuda enim donatio et nuda pactio non obligant aliquem. See also Chapter XVIII.

(*p*) I. Feud. 25.; II. Feud. 2 *sq.*; II. Feud. 7. § 1.

(*q*) Upon homage, v. Reeves, History, I. 227 *sq.*; Phillips, Englische Rechtsgeschichte, II. 208 *sq.*; Bracton 77. 79.: si......seisina non sequatur, homagium effectum non habebit; f. 39 b.:—quia non transfertur per homagium res data.

(*r*) I.e., in relation to the acquisition of property. See also Chapter XI.

([2]) See Blackstone's remarks, Com. II. 311, on the assumed correspondence of the livery of seisin with the investiture, and Reeves's views concerning the difference between the feudal law of England and that of other countries; v. Reeves, I. 44 note b.—*Tr.*

personam, de manu propria vel aliena......in alterius manum, gratuita translatio."

It presupposed a *justa causa:* Justa causa.

"item oportet quod *vestita sit traditio et non nuda*, scilicet quod traditionem præcedat *vera causa vel putativa*, qua transeat dominium" (*s*) (*Cf.* Azo 246 b. and L. 31. D. de adq. rer. dom. 41. 1.).

It gave to the new possessor the same right only which the former one possessed: Effect of traditio.

"item videndum quid transferat qui tradit, et sciendum est quod illud totum (et aliter quam ipse teneat, et seipsum obligare potest) transferat ad eum qui accipit, quod est apud eum qui tradit, ut si quis in fundo dominium habuerit, et merum jus et proprietatem feodi, et liberum tenementum, et usum fructuum et totum, tradendo statim totum transfert ad donatorium ...... Si autem nihil omnino habuerit qui tradit, nec aliquam seisinam, ad eum qui accipit nil transfert, quia dare et transferre non potest nec tradere, id quod non habet. Cum autem dominium tradatur, transfertur ad accipientem tale dominium, quale fuit apud eum qui tradidit"......(*t*) (evidently from L. 20. pr. § 1. l. c.).

The question, which of several conflicting claimants of possession had the better right, is also decided according to Roman rules. If their pretensions Conflicting claims to possession.

(*s*) Bracton 39 b. 41 b. Fleta III. 15. § 4. Nihil interest, adds Bracton f. 40, an ipse dominus per se tradat alicui rem suam, an alius voluntate ipsius, sicut per procuratorem; = L. 9. § 4. D. de adq. rer. dom. 41. 1.; Bracton 40. 43. 44.

(*t*) Bracton 40 b. [This passage of Bracton, which, however, is not quite fully cited in the German edition, and the passage on fol. 161 b. cited by Lord Mansfield (1 Burrow 109) sustain the following version of Reeves I. 304, 305: "If the person making livery had only the usufruct, yet he thereby gave his feoffee a freehold as far as concerned himself and all others who had no right, though *not* as against the true owner. If he had nothing, nothing he could give; yet, if a person was only in possession, let that be as inferior as it might be, it is clearly laid down by Bracton that he could give a precarious fee and freehold by livery." The "good sense" attributed by Lord Tenterden (3 Barn. & Cress. 402) to Lord Mansfield, was in sustaining Bracton's doctrine, viz., that the feoffment of a wrongful possessor may convey a fee simple of wrong, but cannot create such a fee to the true owner's prejudice.—*Tr.*]

were derived from the same person (whether he was the owner or not), preference was given to the oldest traditio according to the verses:

> "*Rem domino vel non domino vendente duobus,*
> *In jure est potior traditione prior.*"

If their claims were derived from different persons, the successor of the true owner was preferred to that of the non dominus, as in L. 31. § 2. in fin. D. de act. emt. et vend. 19. 1.; but if both deduced their rights from non-owners, the earliest possessor had the preference, as in the opinion of Neratius in l.c.:

> "si a duobus non dominis fiat donatio et traditio de eadem re......duobus......,quantum ad donatorios, *ille præfertur, qui prius fuit in seisina*" (*u*).

Conditional and modified donationes.

The subject of *donationes* gives Bracton occasion to speak of the different ways in which the alienation might be affected by condition and modification (modus) (*v*). The modifications of donationes are considered, and classified according to the four kinds of innominate contracts of the Roman law:

> "do ut des, do ut facias,"
> "facio ut des, facio ut facias" (*w*).

The effect of the modification or "modus" was that, in case of non-fulfilment thereof, an action *ex conventione* might be brought for its fulfilment or for the *interesse*. But the revendication of the thing given, which the Roman law allows, is only admitted by Bracton when a resolutory condition to that effect had been made, providing for the contingency of non-fulfilment (*x*). Here he raises the question whether the modification of the donatio affected a third party in posses-

(*u*) Bracton 41. Fleta III. 15. § 8; where the above verses are also found.

(*v*) Bracton 18 b., where the following versus memorialis is found:

"Scito, quod *ut* modus est, *si* conditio, *quia* causa."

(*w*) Bracton, 19, gives the following examples: do tibi Digestum, ut des mihi Codicem; do tibi Codicem, ut facias mihi scribi Digestum; facio tibi domum, ut des mihi Codicem; facio tibi aulam, ut facias mihi cameram.

(*x*) Bracton, 19.—ita quod si dedero vel fecero, tu teneris ad dandum vel faciendum,......sed *tamen ut repetere possim, quod dedi,* si tu non vis facere, quod promisisti (must manifestly mean: ut *non* possim repetere, as in Fleta III. 3. § 4.: *repetere non tamen poterit* quod dedit; likewise Bracton 18,—*revocari non*

sion of the thing, and affirms that it did so in the case in which, in addition to a mere personal obligation between the contractors, the thing itself should be held to be burdened and bound:

> "si dicat donator, do tibi talem rem, ut invenias mihi necessaria, *ex hoc obligatur......non ipsa res......* Si autem sic dicat, quod invenias mihi necessaria *ex re data, ex tali obligatione*, obligatur *tam ipsa res*, quam persona" (*y*).

Conditions.

Conditions "in futurum collatæ" were alone regarded as true conditions, for

> "conditio in præteritum collata infirmat obligationem, vel omnino non differt" (from § 6. J. 3. 15.).

Their different kinds.

Of the different kinds of conditions familiar to us Bracton mentions the following: the conditio potestativa, e.g. "do tibi talem rem, si mihi dederis X," which might also be put in potestate alterius, "si Titius voluerit;" the conditio *casualis*, depending ex insidiis fortunæ, e.g. "si navis ex Asia venierit, si Titius consul factus fuerit;" the *conditio mixta vel disjunctiva*, ex parte potestativa, ex parte casualis; and the *conditio impossibilis*, cui natura impedimento fuerit quod existat, e.g., "si cœlum digito tetigeris," which, if in the positive, nullified the whole proceeding, if in the negative, made it unconditional (*z*). Lastly suspensive and resolutory conditions are broadly distinguished in their effects; by the former "donatio suspenditur, donec conditio existat," by the latter "pura est donatio et perfecta, sed resolvitur sub tali conditione" (*aa*).

---

poterit), sed ad hoc tantum agere possum, quod tu facias, nisi aliter convenerit ab initio. Poterit enim huic donationi sub modo adjici conditio......,si non dederis, vel non feceris......,quod ego repetere possum, quod dedi. Bracton 47 b.

(*y*) Bracton 47. 18 b. Fleta III. 9. § 25.: Ex conditione apposita quandoque obligatur persona, quandoque ipsa res.

(*z*) Bracton 19. 47. 99 b. 100. Si conditio fuerit impossibilis......,non valet donatio et pro non adjecta habetur conditio. This passage is corrupt in its text; either the *non* before *adjecta* must be expunged, as is indeed the case in Fleta III. 9. § 10.: et pro adjecta habebitur conditio, i.e. it has a nullifying force; or after *et* a second *non* must follow: et *non* pro non adjecta habetur conditio, whereby Bracton would deny expressly the Roman doctrine concerning impossible conditions in testaments.

(*aa*) Bracton 47. 19 b. [*Cf.* Reeves I. 294, 295.—*Tr.*]

CHAPTER XIV.

USUCAPIO.

Usucapio.

Difference between the law in Glanville and in Bracton.

LAND could be acquired *per usucaptionem* (*a*), says Bracton, sine titulo et traditione. Prescription was unknown to the old English law and also to Glanville. The latter merely indicates a limitation of actions in the provision that the recognitio de nova disseisina must be brought

> "infra tempus a domino rege et consilio procerum ad hoc constitutum" (*b*).

Bracton, on the contrary, not only makes the rule general

> "quod omnes actiones in mundo infra certa tempora habent limitationem,"

but also connects with it certain legal effects resulting from long possession; effects, which he expresses in the following principle occurring in different forms:

> "*longa possessio parit jus*,"—"longa possessio sufficit pro jure" (*c*).

Prescription in England.

These were beginnings of a prescription. The name usucapio and some of its requisites show that it undoubtedly owed its existence to Roman legal ideas, but, as can be seen from Bracton's short notice, it never passed beyond the limits of the first crude attempts at development. Prescription as a legal institution failed even later to obtain a firm footing in England (*d*).

(*a*) This spelling is always adopted by Bracton.

(*b*) Glanville XIII. 32. 33.

(*c*) Bracton 40. 52. 102 b. 373, etc.

(*d*) At the present day the English law only admits prescription as to certain incorporeal hereditaments; there is no prescription for corporeal things.

Bracton's view of usucapio.

In Bracton usucapio does not appear closely distinguished from the limitation of actions, or at least such is indicated to be the case by the declaration on f. 52 that

> "tempus est......modus adquirendi possessionis, longa enim possessio parit jus possidendi et *tollit actionem vero domino petenti.*"

He considers however the essential element of prescription to lie in acquisition

> "*per longam, continuam et pacificam possessionem* ex diuturno tempore;......*continuam* dico, ita, quod non sit interrupta; interrumpi enim poterit......per denunciationem et impetrationem diligentem,......et per talem interruptionem nunquam adquiret possidens ex tempore liberum tenementum; *pacificam* dico, quia si contentiosa fuerit, idem erit quod prius" (f. 51 b. 52.).

The requisite period of time, during which the possession must have continued, was not definitely fixed, but was left to the discretion of the judges:

> "sed quam longa esse debeat, non definitur a jure, sed ex discretione justiciariorum."

In some passages, a period of ten years—"*post tempus longissimum scilicet decem annorum,*" and as to servitutes a "tempus quod *exedit memoriam,*" are spoken of (*e*). Neither a title nor bona fides was necessary, no regard being paid to the Canon law principle established in 1216,

> "quod nulla valeat præscriptio absque bona fide" (c. 20. X. de præscrip. 2. 26.).

Usucapio, indeed, was even accorded to the disseisor. This is however connected with the peculiar operation and effect which Bracton attributes to it. He considers usucapio to be a means of acquiring not the right of property, but only *rights of possession* (modus adquirendi *possessionis;* adquiritur *possessio* ex tempore etc.) (*f*). In fact its effect, like that of the *rechte*

(*e*) Br. 45 b. 51 b. 52. 53. In one passage f. 422.: longum tempus scilicet X, XX, XXX annos.

(*f*) *Cf.* also the title of chapter 22.: "qualiter adquiritur *possessio* per usucaptionem."

Gewere in the Germanic law (*g*) was only to strengthen the protection of a man's possession. Thus, he who had originally no right of possession obtained a liberum tenementum after a lapse of time per longam possessionem, and this freehold right of possession was protected by all *possessory* legal remedies against all who had a better right, even against the true owner himself on account of his negligence. The latter however did not at all lose his *jus majus;* that could only be extinguished by the loss of his writ of right, the limitation for bringing which was not indeed fixed at any precise number of years (*h*).

ADDITIONAL NOTE TO CHAPTER XIV.

The following references give the ancient limitations of actions for the recovery of land.

Glanville XIII. 35.

Stat. Merton 20 Henry III. c. 8.

Bracton 179, 233, 253 b., 373.

Provisions 43 Henry III., Stat. R. f. 8.

Stat. Marlbridge 52 Henry III. c. 9.

The limitation of primam transfretationem Domini Regis qui nunc est in Vasconiam, given in Stat. Merton c. 8., and that mentioned by Bracton, 179, post ultimum reditum Domini Regis de Britannia in

---

(*g*) *Cf.* O. Stobbe: die Gewere, in Ersch und Gruber: Encyclopædie, 468. [Upon the rechte Gewere or recta possessio of the German feudal law, v. Senkenberg, Corpus Juris Feudalis p. 65. "Qui possessionem rectam (die rechte Gewere) habet alicujus feudi, de quo ab alio controversia movetur, potior erit ad obtinendum, quam qui possessione caret." See also other passages given in the index under the word *Gewere.—Tr.*]

(*h*) Here is the best proof of the relative character of the English rights in things. He who acquired land bona fide had a right of possession against the man from whom the acquisition was made, and against all others who had no better right. Against those who had a better right he acquired a right of possession ex longa possessione, although not having it originally.

Angliam, refer to one and the same voyage of Henry III. to the continent. He returned to England on 1 May, 1230, having while absent been first in Britanny and afterwards in Gascony (see Mathew Paris, Edit. 1640, pp. 365 to 367). Coke, 2 Inst. 95, and Reeves, I. 344 note, appear to have thought that Bracton and the Statute of Merton referred to two distinct voyages. Reeves considers it difficult to account for the want of agreement between Bracton and the statute. —Bracton, in speaking of writs of intrusion f. 160 b., remarks:—quod post longum tempus agi non poterit de *intrusione*, scilicet post *decem annos* vel *duodecim*.—*Translator*.

CHAPTER XV.

SERVITUTES.

Res incorporales.

Predial servitutes.

BRACTON discusses the acquisition of res incorporales in chapter 23. of his second book. For our purposes however the only things of this class which demand attention are predial servitutes, as touching them some general fundamental principles are borrowed from the Roman law.

In the English as in the Roman law, a servitus presupposed a relation existing between two pieces of land:

> "pertinent de fundo ad fundum alicujus proprium."

Rights, which were granted to the person only of their possessor, were not held to be servitutes; it was requisite that

> "domus domui, rus ruri, fundus fundo subjungatur non tantum personæ" (*a*).

Kinds thereof.

The following, for the most part known also to the Roman law, are among the different kinds of servitutes enumerated by Bracton:

The *jus eundi, agendi* (iter, via, actus, without however the technical Roman distinctions), with which the refectio itineris was connected (*b*): "ad viam enim pertinet refectio;"

The *jus aquæ ducendi* (aquæductus),

> "ex fundo alieno et per fundum alienum ad fundum proprium ad irrigandum agrum vel ad alium commodum faciendum,"

which carried with it the right of cleansing the watercourse;

(*a*) Bracton, 53. 221. Fleta IV. 18. § 1. [F. 233: Item aquæ ductus quandoque debetur et datur prædiis, et quandoque personis. Quod vero prædiis datur, persona extincta non extinguitur. Quod autem datur personis, cum personis amittitur, ideo ad nullum transit successorem.—*Tr.*]

(*b*) Bracton, 221 b. 232. Fleta IV. 27. § 1.

that right however being sometimes limited to certain fixed times "nocturnarum vel diurnarum horarum" (*c*);

The *jus fodiendi aurum* (aurifodina), argentum, lapides, arenam, cretam etc.

The right of common of pasture (*communia pasturæ*, and jus pascendi), which Bracton discusses at great length, was for the most part developed independently of the foreign law and in accordance with the wants of the country (*d*).

Acquisition thereof.

The acquisition of servitutes, whether with or without the will of the owner of the servient land, followed the analogy of the acquisition of corporeal things. In the first case, it took place through the owner's voluntary creation or imposition of the servitus, accompanied by a quasi-traditio corresponding to the traditio of a corporeal thing:

> "jura siquidem, cum sint incorporalia, videri non poterunt nec tangi et ideo traditionem non patiuntur sicut res corporales. Oportet igitur ex necessitate, quod in hujusmodi contrahatur donatio ex affectu contrahentium et solo animo et voluntate transferendi et accipiendi, et aspectu rei corporalis cui insunt hujusmodi jura, et *sic quasi possidentur ex fictione juris;*"—

and

> "ita pertinent servitutes alicujus fundo ex constitutione sive ex impositione de voluntate dominorum" (*e*).

Quasi-traditio.

In regard to the requisites of the *quasi-traditio*, Bracton follows the contemporary Roman jurists, and especially Azo. He however deviates from the latter in regard to the manner of practically executing the quasi-traditio. Azo in Cod. de servit. et aqua 3. 34. f. 59. No. 2. says:

> "constituuntur servitutes omnes per traditionem non veram......sed *quasi traditionem*, quæ fit *per patientiam domini, ipso me inducente in possessionem* (but the question is, *how?*)......,et cavet, quod me non impediat utentem." L. 1. § 2. D. de serv. præd. rust. 8. 3.; L. 3. § 2. D. de act. emt. 19. 1.—

(*c*) Bracton, 231 b. 233. Fleta IV. 26. § 1.

(*d*) Bracton, 222–230. Fleta, IV. 18–24.

(*e*) Bracton 52 b. 53. 221.

Bracton on the contrary holds corporal propinquity and the view of the servient land to be sufficient:

> "et sufficit pro traditione *aspectus loci*, in quo hujusmodi jura constituuntur......*et affectus possidendi*, et ex sola voluntate et affectu est quis in possessione."
>
> "Res autem incorporales sicut jura, servitutes, cum loca fuerint determinata, adquiruntur scilicet ex solo aspectu accipientis vel procuratoris sui et possidendi voluntate et affectu" (*f*).

Prescription.

Servitutes might be acquired, without the consent of the owner of the servient land, by prescription,

> "*per longum usum, continuum et pacificum et non interruptum;*"
>
> "ex longo usu, sine constitutione......ex scientia, negligentia et patientia dominorum;"

but it was requisite that the usus should have taken place nec vi, nec clam, nec precario, as in the Roman law. A *longus usus* in this case was only one,

> "qui *excedit memoriam hominum;* tale enim tempus sufficit pro jure (*g*);

a view derived apparently from a mistaken generalisation of L. 3. § 4. D. de aqua. 43. 20. Mutuus dissensus and non usus or negligentia are mentioned as causing the extinction of servitutes. ([1])

(*f*) Bracton 221 b. 225. One passage seems to recall the inducere in possessionem of Azo, viz., f. 225.: donatorius sic per se vel per procuratorem *inducatur in seisinam, quod tenementum videat,* in quo communia conceditur, hoc sufficit pro traditione et statim est in seisina per affectum, et aspectum, vel quasi.—Fleta also, IV. 18. §§ 1. 2.; 20. § 7.

(*g*) Bracton 221. 222 b. 230. Fleta IV. 24. § 6. Azo 59. No. 1. appears to be the authority for the immemorial period of prescription: Nam constituunter servitutes per consuetudinem temporis, *cujus non exstat memoria.*

([1]) See Appendix; note to Chapter XV.—*Tr.*

CHAPTER XVI.

THE LAW OF INHERITANCE.

The law of inheritance.

THE national character of a people impresses itself upon their law of inheritance, and establishes therein settled forms embodying its animating principles, at an earlier period and to a greater extent than in any other province of the law. It is therefore there that the national character offers the most enduring resistance to the introduction of foreign elements into the law. Such was the case in England. As early as the end of the twelfth century the English law of inheritance had become perfected in a manner so peculiarly national, and its main principles so strongly established, that there was little ground left upon which the Roman law could operate with much effect. This was so much the more the case, because it was just in their systems of inheritance that the two laws presented the most marked contrast. Instead of the Roman universal succession according to the will of the testator or the legal provisions for intestacy, the then English system divided the deceased's property into two portions, the one consisting of immovables and the other of movables. For the former the succession was always intestate, testaments not being permitted for immovables in accordance with the maxim:

Law of inheritance in Glanville's time.

"solus deus heredem facere potest non homo" (*a*).

(*a*) Glanville VII. 1. Bracton 62 b. The latter indeed defines hereditas as "successio in universum jus, quod defunctus antecessor habuit," but this is evidently only an explanation of the usual meaning of the Latin term, intended to be understood in a Roman and not in an English sense. [The texts of Glanville and Bracton certainly negative the existence of the testamentary power over land. The power must therefore have been extinct before the end of the reign of Henry II., except in those districts in which it was established upon local usages. But a general power of devising land seems to have existed

While, furthermore, in the Roman law of intestate succession there was no regard paid to sex and priority of birth, and the nearness of the degrees of kindred was in essentials decisive, we find that the English law of succession showed a strong preference for the male line and the eldest born, and entirely excluded ascendants according to the maxim:

"hereditas nunquam ascendit" (*b*).

Influence of the Roman law.

These marked differences did not however prevent some Roman elements from penetrating into and being adopted in the English law of inheritance; a circumstance partially owing to the Church. Such influence, however, affected but few essential points, or matters only indirectly relating to the law of inheritance. Thus the law concerning the legitimacy and bastardy of children as bearing on their capacity to inherit, presents an example of the effects of Roman influence.

Legitimacy and bastardy.

Legitimus heres.

According to the English law, the *legitimus heres* was alone capable of inheriting. The legitimus heres was regularly only he, who was "ex *justis nuptiis* et legitima uxore procreatus." Children so begotten were called, according to a terminology taken from Azo, *liberi legitimi* ET *naturales* (*c*). All not legitimate were comprised under the name of *bastardi*, and their legal condition designated as *bastardia*. Bastards were therefore:

1. The children of concubines, "liberi *naturales tantum et non legitimi*, qui procreantur et nati sunt ex concubina;"
2. Those born before actual marriage or beyond a certain time after it;
3. "Liberi *nec naturales*, *nec legitimi*, qui nati sunt ex prohibito coitu," including spurii, adulterini, and those ex non legitimo matrimonio nati (*d*).

That the last mentioned were still incapable of inheriting in Glanville's time without reference to the bona or mala

---

before the conquest (Hickes Dissert. Epist.) and in the reign of Henry I. (Mad. Exch. (4to.) I. 110–112 notes *l* and *m*).—*Tr.*]

(*b*) Glanville VII. 1. Bracton 62 b.: Descendit jus quasi ponderosum quidquid cadens deorsum......,et nunquam ea via reascendit, qua descendit.

(*c*) Bracton 63. 64. Azo 132 b.

(*d*) Bracton 64. 265. 418. Azo 132 b. Fleta VI. 1. §§ 5. 6.

fides of their parents, is to be concluded from that author's language ("quod ex *legitimo* matrimonio non sit natus") (*e*). But it appears from the statement of the law by Bracton, that before the latter's work was written the English law had accommodated itself to the ordinances of the Church, and expressly recognized the legitimacy of the children of *putative marriages* in accordance with c. 2. X. qui filii. 4. 17., even when the bona fides was only unilateral:

Children of putative marriages.

> "vel ille, qui in facie ecclesiæ legitimus reputatur,...... cum ambo, vir quam uxor, *bona fide* conjuncti, credentes se legitime copulatos esse, cum sint re vera consanguinitate vel affinitate conjuncti vel alio modo, quod matrimonium stare non possit, vel dummodo alter eorum tantum hoc credat" (*f*).

This however presumed that the marriage had not been entered into clandestinely or contra interdictum ecclesiæ as prohibited in c. 3. X. de clandest. desp. 4. 3. (*g*).

Upon this latter point the laws of the Church were willingly acceded to and without hesitation adopted, for no national custom expressly to the contrary had been developed. On the other hand the Church met with violent resistance in its attempt to introduce and establish the *legitimatio per subsequens matrimonium*, sanctioned by its own and the Roman law. Notwithstanding its then power, the Church was unable to supersede the contrary rule of the domestic law, sustained as it was by the opinion of the country. That law regarded the *ante matrimonium natus* as a bastard, notwithstanding the subsequent marriage of his parents, and prohibited him from inheriting their property.

Special bastardy.

> Glanville VII. 15. "Et quidem licet *secundum canones et leges Romanas* talis filius sit legitimus heres, tamen

(*e*) Glanville VII. 13.

(*f*) Bracton 63. Et ad hoc facit decretale cujus verba hæc sunt: "cum inter I. virum et V. mulierem" (in c. 2. X. 4. 17.: T. mulierem) etc., as in c. 2. l. c.

(*g*) Bracton l. c. Vel si inter tales clandestina fuerunt conjugia ab initio, vel contracta contra interdictum ecclesiæ in gradu prohibito etiam ignoranter, soboles de tali conjunctione suscepta *prorsus* illegitima est censenda, de parentum ignorantia nullum habitura subsidium, cum illi taliter contrahendo clandestina conjugia non *ex parte sciente* (sic! instead of expertes scientiæ), vel saltem affectatores ignorantiæ videantur. Verbatim as in c. 3. § 1. X. 4. 3. *Cf.* Fleta I. 14

secundum jus et consuetudinem regni nullo modo tanquam heres in hereditate sustineatur."

Bracton f. 63.: "—ad ea vero, quæ pertinent ad regnum, non sunt legitimi, nec heredes judicantur,...... *propter consuetudinem regni,* quæ se habet in contrarium."

Pope Alexander III. had specially enjoined upon the English Church the maintenance of the Canonical principle in a decretal addressed to the Bishop of Exeter (c. 6. X. qui fil. 4. 17.), which says:

"tanta vis est matrimonii, ut qui antea sunt geniti, post contractum matrimonium legitimi habeantur."

The Church believed that an easier introduction for this principle could be procured, if its courts assumed cognizance of legitimacy as an effect and consequence of marriage in all cases, even when the question arose only incidentally in an action concerning inheritance or property; it thus endeavored to exclude the king's judges from deciding whether the issue was bastard or legitimate and to restrict them to the mere application of its judgment. But this measure served only to increase the violence of the contest. The secular judges adhering to the principle established by the custom of the realm, changed the question of *law* to one of *fact.* Instead of demanding of the Curia Christianitatis whether the issue was bastard or legitimate, they put the question thus:

"utrum fuerit ille natus ante matrimonium contractum vel post?",

and reserved to themselves the deduction of the legal consequences depending upon the decision of this matter of fact (*h*). This excited the displeasure of the clergy to so great an extent that they refused outright to answer a question so specifically framed, alleging conscientious scruples against doing so. The secular judges were however prepared for this contingency. As the question so put was one of fact, framed

(*h*) This appears clearly from Glanville VII. 13-15. [*Cf.* Blackstone, Law Tracts, Introduction to Charters, lxxxi; Beames's note to Glanville 182; Coke, Institutes, II. 97. The date of the decretal of Alexander III. was 1160.—*Tr.*]

merely to ascertain the time when the issue was born, and involved nothing relative to the existence or lawfulness of the marriage itself, they did not hesitate to withdraw it altogether from the clerical jurisdiction, and have it decided by a jurata, like other questions of fact (*i*). The bishops indeed endeavored to have the disputed point decided in their favor at the Parliament of Merton in 1236: but their declaration that they

> "nec voluerunt nec potuerunt sine præjudicio dignitatis ecclesiasticæ respondere ad breve super hujusmodi inquisitione facienda de bastardia,"

and their proposal,

> "quod ad hoc consensum præberent, quod nati ante matrimonium quoad omnia legitimi esse possent, sicut ille qui post,"

served only to elicit the sharp unanimous answer of the barons,

> "quod noluerunt leges Angliæ mutare, quæ usque ad illud tempus usitatæ fuerunt et approbatæ."

It was perhaps due to this resoluteness of the barons, that the clergy receded from their position, for in the same year a compromise was brought about whereby the clerical judges were to continue to inquire into the question of fact whether the birth was before or after marriage, and were to decide that point alone, without touching the question of legitimacy or bastardy (*j*) ([1]).

(*i*) Bracton mentions f. 417 a case of 11 Henry III. (1227), in which Martin de Pateshull, himself a clerk, decided in favor of adopting the jurata. Bracton's own opinion is in its favor.

(*j*) Bracton 417–419.:—mittatur loquela ad ordinarium loci et fiat inquisitio per hæc verba, "utrum vid. talis N. natus fuerit ante matrimonium vel post," et rescribat ordinarius per eadem verba domino regi sine *aliqua cavillatione*. Appeals extra regnum were forbidden and writs of prohibition served to restrain any excesses of ecclesiastical jurisdiction. Bracton 404 b. 405.

([1]) According to Selden the words "*anno eodem*" in Bracton, f. 417 line 9, are an error for "*anno regni Henrici filii regis Johannis xviii;*" such being the reading of the record which Bracton appears to have transcribed almost verbatim. Blackstone, therefore, holds that the settlement of the dispute concerning special bastardy must have been at the Parliament of Tewksbury, 18 Henry III, 1234. (See also Bracton, 96). The proceedings at the Parliament of Merton

Proof of legitimacy.

The Roman presumption, *pater est quem nuptiæ demonstrant*, was valid in England, being thus expressed:

"legitimus filius est quem nuptiæ demonstrant,"

or thus:

"nuptiæ probant filium esse" (*k*).

There was however a deviation from the Roman rule in one respect, namely, that there was no definite term fixed for the continuance of the presumption after a marriage had ceased to exist, it being left to the decision of each particular case to determine it (*l*). Only in cases where the husband's paternity was physically impossible (absence, impotence, sickness etc.), could proof of bastardy be dispensed with as in L. 6. D. de hiis qui. 1. 6.; but in such cases it was not excluded by the previous recognition of the issue by the alleged father. On the other hand, where the husband could by any possibility be the true father, any doubt concerning the issue's legitimacy was removed by his recognition, either impliedly given by rearing and educating the child as his own, or expressly made before witnesses (as in Nov. 117. c. 2.) (*m*).

Supposititious children.

With the foregoing should be connected the proceeding for preventing the fraudulent substitution of children by an examination, per legales et discretas

(*k*) Bracton 6. 63. 70. 417 b. *et al.* Fleta I. 14. § 1. Glanville VII. 12 in fin.

(*l*) Bracton 417 b. Item si inquiratur per quantum tempus natus fuerit post inhumationem patris......,ita quod non possit esse veresimile, quod sit filius talis. 419 b. 70.: computato tempore, scilicet a tempore, quo dicebat se concepisse, et etiam a morte viri usque ad diem pariendi.

(*m*) Bracton 6. 63 b. Si autem violenta præsumtio se faciat in contrarium,...... ut ecce maritus probetur propter aliquam infirmitatem vel frigiditatem vel aliam impotentiam coeundi per multum tempus non concubuisse cum uxore, vel si probetur, quod extra regnum. ....per biennium et ultra longe extiterit, et quod vehementur præsumi possit, quod ad uxorem accessum habere non potuit, et cum redierit, pregnantem invenerit, vel parvum habentum anniculum, sive talem advocaverit et nutrierit, vel non......,erit talis filius a successione repellendus. Bracton 5. 278. 418.

must therefore be considered an unsuccessful attempt on the part of the bishops to reopen the question. Blackstone, Introduction to Charters, lxxxiii; Selden, Titles of Honor, B. 2. c. 5. § 23. In regard to the exceptional effect of the Canon law rule, in the case of *bastard eigné* and *mulier puisné*, see Blackstone Com. II. 248 and Coke upon Littleton 244.—*Tr.*

mulieres, of the woman alleged to be pregnant, and by placing her person in custody. The legal provisions upon this subject bear so strong a resemblance to the pretorian edict de inspiciendo ventre D. 25. 4, that they must be regarded as being taken from it (*n*).

Right of representation: — uncle and nephew.

The order of succession according to the English law was influenced by the Roman in one point only. In my opinion the gradually established recognition of the so-called right of representation in the succession of descendants must be referred to legal views derived from the Roman law and from the Church. Upon this turned the important disputed question, whether the nephew or the uncle should inherit in the case where the deceased's surviving issue at the time of his death consisted of a younger son and of a grandson by an elder son who had died before him (*o*).

In Glanville's time while some considered the uncle to be the true heir, in consequence of the elder brother never having lived to have the inheritance cast upon him, others regarded the nephew as such,

> "cum ille ex filio progenito exierit et de corpore suo extiterit heres in totum jus, quod pater suus, si adhuc viveret, haberet."

Glanville himself took the latter view, at least in the case where the elder son had not been provided for (forisfamiliatus) by his father (*p*). He little dreamed of the practical import-

(*n*) Br. 69–71. The Writ runs: Rex Vicecom. salutem. Præcipimus tibi quod omni dilatione et occasione præposita, venire facias coram te......A., quæ fuit uxor B., et quæ se facit pregnantem, et......facias eam videri per legales et discretas mulieres, per quas melius veritas sciri poterit, et diligenter tractari a mulieribus prædictis per ubera et per ventrem, modis omnibus, quibus inde melior possit certiorari, utrum pregnans sit nec ne; et si......mulieres viderint, quod pregnans sit, vel inde dubitaverint, tunc illam poni facias in castro nostro tali, et ita, quod nulla domicella, quæ pregnans sit vel alia, de qua suspicio haberi possit alicujus falsitatis faciendæ sit cum ea, et in castro illo moram faciat, quousque de partu suo constare possit.

(*o*) The question might also arise in regard to the inheritance of an eldest brother. [Upon the question whether the uncle or nephew was the true heir, there are cases of interest in Rot. Cur. Reg. I. pp. ix, 358, 359; II. 48, 49, 51, 189.—*Tr.*]

(*p*) Glanville VII. 3. Ita dico, si pater suus non fuerit ab avo suo forisfamiliatus.

ance which this question would soon assume in the contest for the throne between King John and his nephew Arthur of Brittany, in which the former was not, for this reason, looked upon as the mere usurper he has since usually been considered (*q*). While the case of the Crown actually resulted in the uncle's obtaining the throne, the legal judgment of the nation and that of the judges, who were familiar with the Roman law, must have strongly leaned towards the better right of the nephew, for at least as early as Bracton's time the right of representation in the person of the grandson was recognized, and has never been doubted since (*r*). Evidently however from a fear of putting in question the king's title to the crown, the rejected doctrine was so far adopted that, when the uncle had once become seized of the inheritance, the nephew could not make good his better title by way of action. For, notwithstanding the latter's being recognized as the true heir de jure, the uncle was protected in his seisin, as in a bonorum possessio, against the nephew, on account of the precedent in what was called the *king's case* (*s*).

Partition.

The communio existing between coheirs (coheredes, participes) was dissolved by a proceeding in partition (*t*), which was copied without doubt from the Roman judicium familiæ herciscundæ. As in the latter,

(*q*) John was the youngest son of Henry II.; Geoffrey of Brittany, Arthur's father, and John's elder brother, died before his father, and therefore before Richard I., whose death placed the title to the crown in dispute. King John's title appears not to have been disputed in England. [See Reeves I. 42.—*Tr.*]

(*r*) Bracton 64 b. [The reference on p. 28 to this note should be to the one following.—*Tr.*]

(*s*) Br. 267 b.: cum autem avunculus *prius fuerit in possessione* hereditatis......et nepos petat versus eum *de seisina patris*......,locum non habebit assisa, sed tantum breve de recto per quod, si compertum fuerit, quod nepos heres fuerit propinquior et justior propter juris prærogativam, *tamen nihil capiat per judicium propter casum regis, qui hucusque se habuit in contrarium*, et remanebit semper judicium in suspenso. 268.:—et sic remanebit avunculus semper in seisina, quia judicium remanebit in suspenso *propter casum regis super jure*. 327 b.:—quamdiu *casus regis duraverit, nunquam* ad judicium procedetur. It is remarkable that even English legal historical writers have not observed this peculiarity. Reeves, I. 310, is entirely inaccurate. [Upon the death of Arthur's sister Eleanor, both titles to the crown were united in Henry III., and there ceased to be any reason of state for favoring the uncle. Eleanor died in 1241. See ante p. 28.—*Tr.*]

(*t*) Parceners, as a rule, were females.

the actio was *mixta*, and "uterque actor, uterque reus." As there, the respective rights of co-inheritance must be previously settled (*u*). The partition was made in the following manner. An appraisement was first made, and then a division into the proper number of equal shares. These latter were in general distributed by lot, and the *assignatio partium*, corresponding to the adjudicatio of the Roman proceeding, was pronounced in the Curia Regis (*v*).

Testaments.

So much for the law of inheritance and intestate succession.—With testaments relating to movables Bracton had no occasion to deal closely, for testamentary causes were left to the cognizance of the courts Christian. The form of making testaments was far from following the strict rules of the Roman law, as we learn from the concurrent though scant remarks of Glanville, Bracton and Fleta. Thus, evidently from a consideration of the Canon law c. 10. 11. X. de test. 3. 26., it sufficed to have but two witnesses:

> "ad minus coram duobus......viris legalibus et honestis, clericis vel laicis *ad hoc specialiter convocatis*" (*w*).

Donatio mortis causa.

On the other hand Bracton regards the *donatio mortis causa* as a distinct legal institution, belonging to the jurisdiction of the lay courts; a doctrine undoubtedly taken from the Roman law (*x*). Bracton, like Ulpian in L. 2. D. de don. mort. caus. 39. 6., divides this donation into three kinds:

> "una, cum quis nullo presentis mortis periculi metu conterritus, sed *sola cogitatione mortalitatis* donat; alia, cum quis imminente *periculo mortis commotus ita donat, ut statim fiat accipientis*, tertia, si quis commotus periculo non dat, ut statim fiat accipientis, *sed tunc demum, cum mors fuerit insecuta*."

(*u*) Bracton 71 b.–77.

(*v*) Bracton 75 b. Fortunam faciunt judicem, ut quilibet habeat partem illam, quæ per sortem ei accideret; evidently after L. 3. C. de caduc. 6. 43.

(*w*) Bracton 61. In one passage (354 b.) the seven witnesses are mentioned. *Cf.* Glanville VII. 6.; Fleta II. 57. § 12.

(*x*) Bracton 60. Fleta II. 57. § 1., identifies donationes mortis causa with testaments. Contrahitur etiam obligatio ex testamento, quæ morte confirmatur.

In accordance with LL. 2.—6. l. c. other perils besides that of immediate death might be motives for the donation:

> "mortis causa donare licet, non tantum infirmæ valitudinis causa, sed periculi......ab hoste vel a prædonibus, vel ob hominis potentis crudelitatem vel odium, aut causa navigationis vel peregrinationis imminente, aut si quis fuerit per insidiosa loca iturus, hæc enim omnia instans periculum demonstrant."

The failure of the donation if the donee died first, and its revocation, when the danger of the donor's death had passed away, follow as a matter of course:

> "in se tacitam habent conditionem, ut hujusmodi donationes revocentur, si ægrotus convaluerit...... Si autem sic donetur mortis causa, ut nullo casu revocetur, causa donandi magis est quam mortis causa donatio" (from L. 27. D. de mortis causa don. 39. 6.).

Finally, the rule in L. 26. D. hoc tit. was also adopted, for

> "si duo, qui sibi invicem mortis causa donaverint, pariter decesserint, neutrius heres repetet, quia neuter alterum supervixit" (*y*).

(*y*) Bracton 60. Fleta l. c.

CHAPTER XVII.

DOWER.

It has already been intimated that "*dos secundum consuetudinem Anglicanam*" was not the Roman institution, and that the English dos should rather be compared to the *doarium* (*Witthum*) of the Germanic legal authorities (*a*). But as in England dower was

Dos in the English and in the Roman law.

> "quod liber homo dat sponsæ suæ ad ostium ecclesiæ propter nuptias futuras et onus matrimonii,"

the comparison with the Roman donatio propter nuptias readily suggested itself; and as the principles of the Roman dos had an application to the donatio propter nuptias, it may be explained how, notwithstanding the difference between the Roman and the English dotal law, individual technical terms were transferred from the former to the latter. On the subject of dos, there are more Romanisms to be found in Fleta than even in Bracton. Both distinguish between *dos profectitia*,

Dos in Bracton and Fleta.

> "quæ datur a patre vel matre vel alio parente in ipso contractu pro filia maritanda,"

and *dos adventitia*,

> "quæ ab aliis datur, quam a patre, sive parens sit sive extraneus;"

(*a*) Glanville VI. 1. *Dos duobus* modis dicitur, dos vulgariter etc. VII. 1. In alia acceptione accipitur *dos secundum leges Romanas*. Bracton 92 *sq*. Dos is to be understood in the English sense in the decretal c. 6. X. de don. inter. vir. 4. 20, which says in the conclusion by way of explanation: "Illud te nolumus ignorare, quod *uxor dare dicitur viro dotem*, vir autem uxori donationem facere propter nuptias secundum legitimas sanctiones." [This decretal was, it appears, addressed to Scotland and relates to the Scotch terce, which corresponds to the English dower. Upon the subject of dower in Bracton see Long, 99-104.—*Tr*.]

a division clearly inappropriate for the English dos. [1] They also mention a "*dos parapherna*,"

> "quæ sit juxta vel præter dotem" (*b*) [2].

Fleta furthermore adopts the distinction between *dos æstimata* and *inæstimata*, in the first of which

> "tam lucrum quam damnum pertinet ad maritum sicut ad emptorem."

Fleta even mentions the period of one year for the restitution of a dos consisting of movables (vestimentis, jocalibus, pecunia) where the marriage had been dissolved, a thing which though obtaining in the Roman law could hardly have been practically applicable in England. (*c*).

Actio dotis.

In suing for dower the validity of the marriage might be called in question, e.g. when two or more women made claim each to be the true wife (*d*). The decision of this incidental question was assigned to the courts Christian, and the principal action was in the mean time suspended. In such cases the clerical courts do not seem to have been entirely clear as to how they should proceed in making their inquisition, for we find in Bracton a curious account of their obtaining advice from the king's judges in regard to the practical course which they should adopt (*e*).

(*b*) Bracton 92 b. Fleta V. 23. ⸹ 4. "alia *perfectiva* (*sic!*); alia *adventiva*". ⸹ 6. Habet autem paraferna privilegium ad instar dotis.

(*c*) Fleta l. c. ⸹ 9. [*Cf.* L. un. ⸹ 7. C. de rei ux. act. 5. 13.—*Tr.*]

(*d*) Bracton, 302, 306, 308, uses the expressions *possessio viri*, *seisita esse de viro*, in this connection. These expressions are manifestly of Canon law origin, and suffice to show that a *possession* of marriage formed part of the doctrine of Canonists in that day. *Cf.* Bruns, R. d. Besitzes, 191 *sq.* [*Cf.* Rotteck & Welcker, Staats-Lexicon, Ed. 3. Vol. 9. p. 7.—*Tr.*]

(*e*) Bracton 302 b. 307. instances such a consultatio: Rex tali episcopo sal.

---

[1] The context of these passages is as follows: et dotis species sunt duae, alia profectitia, alia adventitia. Profectitia dici poterit, etc......,*et terra sic data dici poterit maritagium*, et patrimonium mulieris...... *Item adventitia dos dici poterit maritagium.*—See Reeves, I. 297.- *Tr.*

[2] Concerning dos profectiva v. L. 5. D. de jure dotium 23. 3.; dos adventitia, v. Pothier, Pandectæ, Lib. 23. Tit. 3. Num. VII; parapherna, v. ibid. Num. LIV, and L. 9. ⸹ 2. D. l. c. By the law of Normandy the wife had a paraphernal; "les biens paraphernaux s'entendent des meubles servant a l'usage de la femme, comme lits, robes, linges;" v. Pannier, Ruines de la Coutume de Normandie, 80, 81.—*Tr.*

Cum inter A. petentem et B. tenentem coram Justic. nostris de banco contentio dotis verteretur et......ex parte B. eidem A. objiceretur, quod tali viro non fuisset legitimo matrimonio copulata, et tandem ad episc. Wigorn......esset demandata inquisitio facienda; idem episc. nos consuluit qualiter in dicta inquis. facienda esset procedendum. Cujus consultationi *secundum consuetudinem regni Angliæ* sic duximus respondendum,......quod convocatis, convocandis......,sic procedat, quod inprimis denunciare faciat tenenti, quod sit ad certum diem certo loco dictura contra matrimonia si voluerit, et sive tunc venerit sive non, testes, quos mulier......produxerit, admittat, ob contumaciam mulieris alterius, quæ non venerit. *Et veritate absque juris magna solennitate quasi summatim inquisita,* mandatur inquisitio domino regi etc. The conclusion is remarkable for its intimation of the proceeding's being summary. [See the translator's addition to note (*f*) p. 43.—*Tr.*]

CHAPTER XVIII.

THE LAW OF OBLIGATIONS.

BRACTON goes only superficially into the law of obligations. The extent of his commentary upon it, however, is in corresponding proportion to the limited importance, which the English in his time still attributed to movable property and its relation to the law. The little which he gives upon this head is found in connection with his commentary upon actions in the first tract of the third book; a juxtaposition, which he justifies by adopting Azo's explanation that the relation between obligations and actions was that of mothers and daughters (*a*). Emptio and locatio alone have obtained special places in his work, those being assigned to them under the head of causæ adquisitionis rerum dominii.

Law of obligations.

Bracton's notion of an obligation is derived from pr. J. de obligationibus 3. 13, and L. 3. pr. D. de A. and O. 44. 7.; he says

Definition of obligatio.

> "est enim obligatio juris vinculum, quo necessitate adstringimur ad aliquid dandum vel faciendum."

The four sources which he assigns for the origin of obligations are also those of the Roman law, viz., Contract, *quasi*-Contract, Delict, and *quasi*-Delict (*b*).

Origin of obligations.

The old English law did not give binding force and legal validity to the mere intention of contracting, however it might be expressed. It only protected conventions, and actions were only maintainable upon them, when they were either partially per-

Contracts. Old English law thereof.

(*a*) Bracton 99. Videndum est, unde actio oriatur? et sciendum est, quod ex obligationibus præcedentibus, tanquam a *matre filia*. Obligatio autem, quæ est *mater actionis* etc. *Cf.* Azo f. 254 b. No. 7.: de obligationibus, tanquam *matribus* earum (actionum).

(*b*) Bracton ibid. Est enim obligatio, quasi contra ligatio, et quatuor habet species, quibus contrahitur.

formed, or were made in solemn form, i.e. by a written charter under seal, carta sigillata, cyrographum (for chirographum). All other conventions were called *pacta nuda*, and the king's judges could not take cognizance of their violation or non-fulfilment, according to the principle, evidently borrowed from the Roman law, that

"*ex nudo pacto non oritur actio*,"

although the courts Christian might enforce them by inflicting penance

"propter fidei læsionem vel transgressionem."

For, says Glanville

> "privatas conventiones non solet Curia domini Regis tueri, et de talibus contractibus......se non intromittit Curia" (*c*).

Such ideas had many points of contact with the Roman law, and its distinction between actionable and non-actionable conventions. Especially did the English lawyer find pertinent analogies for his peculiar ideas and views in the doctrine of *stipulations*, which the then Civilian school taught as still practically applicable law. The peculiar characteristics of stipulations, their formality, their being clothed in solemn fixed words, the actual presence of the contractors regularly requisite, the strong legal protection afforded by the actions maintainable upon them, all harmonized with the provisions of the English law concerning formal conventions. If we also bear in mind the conformity between writing and stipulation, which at that period already existed in the Civil law, we can readily understand how the principles of the Roman stipulation easily came to be thought applicable by English lawyers. When therefore Bracton and Fleta, in discussing the law of contracts, treat of stipulations at great length, it does not indeed follow that the phrases, "dabis? dabo," "promittis? promitto," mentioned by them, were legal forms used in the actual business of life; but what they say *does* show that they found general rules in the doctrine of stipulations upon which they might reason with applicability to the solemn English conventions upon

Comparison with the Roman law.

(*c*) Glanville X. 18.; X. 8. 12. [*Cf.* Reeves I. 159–169. —*Tr.*]

which actions were maintainable, and that they have therefore reproduced them (*d*).

Pacta nuda; pacta vestita.

In the English law there was thus no room for the Roman law distinction of contractus and pacta. That circumstance, however, neither prevented the English lawyers from adopting a distinction of *pacta nuda* and *pacta vestita*, derived from the same source, for the purpose of discriminating between the non-actionable and the actionable conventions of their own law ([1]), nor deterred them from borrowing from the then Civilian school its list of the different *vestimenta pactorum.* The vestimenta pactorum are enumerated by Bracton in the following versus memoriales:

> "*Re, verbis, scripto, consensu, traditione*
> *Junctura, vestes sumere pacta solent*" (*e*).

The most striking of these are *traditio* and *junctura.* Traditio is here, however, only another expression for Azo's *rei interventus:*

> "ut in contractibus innominatis (says Azo), qui ab initio nullam dant actionem, sed *re postea interveniente et tradita*, competit actio" (*f*).

Junctura is thus described:

> "ut si plura pacta de eadem re deducantur in stipulationem......,si in continenti adjiciantur......,insunt contractibus et dant legem eisdem" (*g*),

and corresponds to the *cohærentia contractuum*, found in Azo referring to pacta adjecta (*h*).

(*d*) The parallelism of stipulation and writing is especially referred to in the following passage, Bracton 100.:—et quod *per scripturam fieri possit stipulatio......* videtur, quia si scriptum fuerit in instrumento aliquem promisisse, perinde habetur, *ac si interrogatione præcedente responsum sit.* The English donatio is also often compared to stipulation; e.g. f. 15 b.: item oportet, quod certa verba interveniant donationi congrua, sicut et stipulationi.

(*e*) Bracton 16 b.

(*f*) Azo in Cod. de pact. f. 17. No. 5.

(*g*) Bracton 16 b. 100 b.; *cf.* Fleta II. 60. § 2.

(*h*) Azo in Cod. de pact. f. 17. n. 3 [where Azo says: vestitur aut pactus sex modis, re, verbis, consensu, litteris, contractus coherentia, rei interventu.—*Tr.*]

([1]) *Cf.* Spence, I. 186 note *f.*—*Tr.*

The place of Verbal obligations (stipulations) is thus clearly indicated: *verba* were words reduced to writing. The *Real* contracts of the Roman law very naturally found an easy and early reception into a law, which had not developed rules of its own in such matters. Even in Glanville we find that the commentary upon "causa mutui, commodati, pignoris," is chiefly made up of Roman principles, while Bracton's exposition of this class of contracts is nothing but an almost literal extract from the corresponding titles of the Institutes. As what Bracton says concerning stipulations is also copied from the same source, it will suffice, instead of any farther discussion of either of these divisions of obligations, to compare the following extracts with the Roman texts.

Verbal obligations (stipulations).

Real contracts.

Extracts from Bracton relating to stipulations and *Real* contracts.

BRACTON Lib. III. tract. 1. c. 2.

§ 1. *Re* autem contrahitur obligatio veluti in *mutui datione*, quæ consistit in rebus, quæ pondere, numero, mensura sunt; pondere, sicut in rebus quæ ponderantur, numero, sicut pecunia numerata......,mensura, sicut in oleo, vino, frumento. Quæ res autem in appendendo, numerando et metiendo in hoc dantur, ut statim fiant accipientium, quia mutuum proprie dicitur id, quod ex meo tuum fit (*i*) (= pr. J. 3. 14.)...... *Hiis* autem (*j*), cui res aliqua utenda datur, re obligatur, quæ *commodata* est; sed magna differentia est inter mutuum et commodatum, quia is, qui rem commodatam accepit, ad ipsam restituendam tenetur vel ejus precium, si forte incendio, ruina, naufragio aut latronum vel hostium incursu, consumpta fuerit vel deperdita, substracta vel ablata (*k*). Et qui rem

---

(*i*) Br. 99. Fleta II. 56. § 5. Glanville X. 3.

(*j*) Evidently instead of *Is* autem, as also in Fleta l. c.

(*k*) Also in Fleta II. 56. § 5. This passage does not appear to agree with what is said below concerning liability for vis major. We must either consider *nisi culpa intervenerit* to be understood, or else hold it to be an echo of the older English law, which held the commodatarius liable for casus. Glanville X. 13.: Si autem res interierit vel perdita fuerit *quocunque modo* in tua custodia, om-

utendam accepit, non sufficit ad rei custodiam, quod talem diligentiam adhibeat, qualem suis rebus propriis adhibere solet, si alius eam diligentius potuit custodire. Ad vim autem majorem vel casus fortuitos non tenetur quis, nisi culpa sua intervenerit, ut si rem sibi commodatam domi secum detulerit cum peregre profectus fuerit et illam incursu hostium vel prædonum, vel naufragio amiserit, non est dubium, quin ad rei restitutionem teneatur (= § 2. J. 3. 14.)...... Is apud quem *res deponitur*, re obligatur, et de ea re, quam accepit, restituenda tenetur et etiam ad id, si quid in re deposita dolo commiserit. Culpæ autem nomine non tenetur, sc. desidiæ vel negligentiæ, quia, qui negligenti amico rem custodiendam tradit, sibi ipsi et propriæ fatuitati hoc debet imputare (= § 3. J. l. c.). Creditor, qui *pignus accepit*, re obligatur, et ad illam restituendam tenetur; et cum hujusmodi res in pignus data sit utriusque gratia sc. debitoris, quo magis pecunia ei crederetur, et creditoris, quo magis ei in tuto sit creditum, sufficit ad illius rei custodiam diligentiam exactam adhibere, quam si præstiterit et rem casu amiserit, securus esse possit, nec impedietur creditum petere (= § 4. J. l. c) (*l*).

§ 2. *Verbis contrahitur obligatio* per *stipulationem*. Est enim stipulatio quædam verborum conceptio, quæ consistit ex interrogatione et responsione, ut si dicatur: promittis? promitto; dabis? dabo; fidejubes? fidejubeo (= pr. § 1. J. 3. 15.; L. 5. § 1. D. de verb. obl. 45. 1.). Et omnis talis stipulatio aut fit pure, aut in diem, aut sub conditione...... Sed si dies adjiciatur, quo solvi debeat, statim debetur, sed peti non poterit ante diem, nec etiam eo die, quia totus is dies relinquitur arbitrio solventis, nec vero certum erit, eo die solutum non esse, priusquam dies præterierit; nec eodem modo recte petit quis, si quis hoc anno vel mense dare stipulatus est, nisi omnibus partibus præteritis anni vel mensis (= § 2. J. l. c.) (*m*).

---

nino teneris ad rationabile pretium mihi restituendum. Glanville here asks the question: sed sub qua vel cujus probatione probandum? From this and other doubtful points in Glanville it can be seen how the Roman law easily came to be adopted in these matters. [See Appendix; note to Chapter XVIII.—*Tr.*]

(*l*) Fleta II. 56. § 6–9.

(*m*) Bracton speaks of the computation of time, leap year etc. f. 264. 359. 360.

§§ 3 and 4. reproduce §§ 4, 6 and 7. J. 3. 15.

§ 5. Item *loca* deducuntur in stipulationem, ut si dicas *existens Oxonii, hodie Londonii dare spondes?* talis stipulatio erit inutilis, nisi tempus, quo fieri possit, adjiciatur (in stipulatione), quia omnino erit impossibile (= § 5. J. l. c.), ac si quis rem promitteret, quæ in rerum natura non esset......vel si rem sacram vel publicam, quæ non est in alicujus bonis. Item si quis stipulatus fuerit, qui alium daturum vel facturum promiserit, quam eum qui in potestate sua extiterit, vel si quis ad ea, quæ interrogatus fuerit, non responderit, nec secundum quod interrogatus fuerit......,vel si unus pure, et alius sub conditione, stipulatio non valebit. Item erit inutilis, si quis ita stipulatus fuerit: si navis venerit de Asia, hodie dare spondes? quia præpostere concepta est; tamen licet præpostera fuerit, non erit rejicienda (= §§ 1. 2. 14. J. 3. 19.).

§§ 6. and 7. correspond to J. 3. 18. and § 18. J. 3. 19. (*n*).

§ 8. In fine autem videndum, quis non possit stipulari nec promittere......,et sciendum, quod mutus nec stipulari potest, nec promittere, cum loqui non possit, nec verba stipulationi congruentia proferre; quod quidem in surdo exceptum est (sic! evidently for receptum), quia is, qui stipulatur verba promittentis, et is, qui promittit, verba stipulantis audire oportet, nisi sit, qui dicat, quod hoc facere possunt per nutus et per scripturam (= § 7. J. 3. 19.) (*o*).

What Bracton says of the so-called "Literal" obligation (*obligatio per scripturam*), is nearly connected with stipulation. The latter was, indeed, in England obligatio per scripturam. He says

Obligatio per scripturam.

(*n*) Fleta II. 56. §§ 9–17.

(*o*) We see how here too the Roman law was remodelled for practical use. The same occurs in regard to § 19. J. 3. 19. concerning stipulations in favor of a third person, which Bracton reproduces as follows: Inventæ sunt hujusmodi stipulationes,......ut unusquisque habeat et sibi adquirat, quod sua interest, si contra ea agatur, quæ in stipulationem deducuntur. Et si res in stipulatione deducta *alii detur nihilominus intererit stipulatoris, quia ille qui promisit tenebitur ad interesse, vel ad pœnam,* si pœna fuerit in stipulationem deducta; v. also Fleta II. 56. § 20.—The stipulation of the pœna was not therefore considered absolutely necessary.

> "per scripturam obligatur quis, ut si quis scripserit alicui si debere, sive pecunia numerata sit, sive non, obligatur ex scriptura, *nec habebit exceptionem non numeratæ pecuniæ* contra scripturam;"

he therefore expressly rejects the Roman law in regard to written acknowledgments of indebtment. It is to be remarked that the principle which excluded the exceptio non numeratæ pecuniæ applied not merely to the obligatio per scripturam, but to every other written and sealed contract (*p*).

Consensual contracts.

The Roman *Consensual contracts* were least of all suited to the English law of contracts, since there was no outward difference between them and English nuda pacta. It is true that Bracton expressly mentions them (*q*), naming emptio, locatio, societas, mandatum, but discussing only the two first at any length, and not under the head of obligations. These contracts seem, however, to be referred to in this connection rather for the theoretical completeness of the system of obligations than for practical reasons.

Emptio.

This is confirmed by what Bracton says concerning emptio, by which it appears that that contract was *not at all a true Consensual contract* in the English law. For, the emptio was not perfected,

> "cum de pretio convenerit inter contrahentes,"

unless, *at the same time* either

> "*arrarum nomine* (a venditore) aliquid receptum fuerit, quia, quod arrarum nomine datum, est argumentum emptionis et venditionis contractæ,"

or,

> "*pretium solutum* fuerit vel *ejus pars et traditio subsequuta*,"

or, in the case the contract was concluded *in writing*,

> "(scriptura) fuerit partibus tradita et absoluta."

(*p*) Bracton 100 b. *Cf.* Glanv. X. 13. Si vero cartam illam ab initio advocavit is, contra quem producitur ad debitum aliquid probandum, tunc juxta cartæ illius tenorem tenebitur ipse debitor creditori satisfacere. [*Cf.* J. 3. 21.—*Tr.*]

(*q*) Bracton 100 b., makes here the remark, quod in his contractibus nominatis uterque obligatur alteri......,et si non a principio tamen postea potest uterque incipere alteri obligari ratione expensarum et hujusmodi. *Cf.* § 2. J. 3. 22. He also calls these contracts bonæ fidei contractus.

That is to say, the emptio remained nudum pactum when it had not been reduced to writing in proper form, or had not been at least partially fulfilled (*r*). After the contract was perfected, if one of the parties failed to comply with it, the other could not, as a rule, recede from it, but had his remedy in an action for its fulfilment.

> "Nec poterit postea aliquis contrahentium a contractu resilire, prætextu pretii non soluti in parte vel in toto, sed agere poterit venditor ad recuperandum id, quod de pretio defuerit, sed non ad *ipsam* (here is manifestly wanting *rem*, which is found in Fleta) *rehabendam.*"

In the opposite case, i.e. as long as the contract was considered to remain nudum pactum merely:

> "locus erit pœnitentiæ et impune recedere possunt partes contrahentes a contractu" (*s*) (*cf.* pr. J. 3. 23.).

This right to withdraw was accorded to both parties by the English as by the Roman law in the case "cum solæ arræ datæ sunt," the buyer losing the arra and the seller double the arra:

> "emptor......*perdat quod dedit*,......venditor......quod arrarum nomine receperit, emptori restituat duplum."

The *buyer's* right to withdraw was recognized from ancient times, but neither the corresponding right of the seller nor the indemnity for its exercise was definitely settled in Glanville's day. Glanville asks the question:

> "si autem venditor recedere voluerit,......quæro, utrum sine pœna id facere possit?"

and answers it in the negative:

> "quia tunc videretur in hoc melioris conditionis venditor quam emptor."

He propounds but gives no answer to this other question:

> "quod si impune id fieri nequit, quam pœnam inde præstabit?"

(*r*) Bracton 61 b. Fleta II. 58. Glanville X. 14.: Perficitur autem emptio ......ex quo de pretio inter contrahentes convenit; ita tamen, quod *secuta fuerit rei .....traditio, vel quod pretium fuerit solutum totum sive pars*, vel saltem quod *arræ inde fuerint datæ et receptæ.*

(*s*) Bracton 61 b. Glanville X. 14.

At a later period the Roman law was received upon this point, and the question settled in accordance with it (*t*).

Its requisites.

As a requisite of the emptio Bracton mentions particularly a "certum pretium." This he holds might also exist when the price was fixed "quanti talis æstimaverit," if an æstimatio really followed. Otherwise, the sale was null, "quasi nullo pretio definito," as in § 1. J. l. c. In regard to the *periculum rei emptæ*, the Roman rule did not apply, but that of the old English law:

"*periculum......generaliter illum respicit, qui rem tenet*" (*u*).

Hence Bracton is enabled to apply, in nearly the same words, to the seller what is said of the buyer in § 3. J. l. c. (*v*).

Conditional sales are mentioned by Bracton, particularly those spoken of in 4. J. l. c.,

"ut, si talis res empta intra certum diem emptori placuerit, sit ei empta aureis tot,"

with which he connects the pactum displicentiæ (mentioned by Glanville also):

"si displicuerit emptori, restituatur" (²).

Locatio conductio.

The contract of locatio conductio is treated of by Bracton at less length. The position of the contractors is thus explained:

"locator tenetur obligatus rem locatam ad usum dare; et conductor tenetur mercedem solvere."

The right of the locator over the invecta and illata as pledges is also recognized:

"si res immobilis locata fuerit,......sicut domus......,

(*t*) Glanville X. 14. Bracton 62. Fleta II. 58. § 5. [According to the Regiam Majestatem double the Earnest was forfeited; see Beames's Glanville, 269 note 1.—*Tr.*]

(*u*) Glanville X. 14.

(*v*) Bracton 62.—Ut si bos venditus, mortuus fuerit ante traditionem, vel ædes incendio consumptæ, vel fundus vi fluminis......ablatus,......totum periculum pertineat ad *venditorem*, at contrario vero videtur, quod si post emptionem, ante traditionem, fundo vendito aliquid per alluvionem......accreverit, quod commodum ad *venditorem* pertinebit...... Commodum ejus esse debebit, cujus est periculum. Fleta II. 58. § 8.

(²) *Cf.* L. 3. D. de cont. empt. 18. 1.—*Tr.*

> omnia *invecta et illata......pro mercede......*pignori sunt annexa" (3).

Finally, we find repeated the liability of the conductor, laid down in § 5. J. 3. 24., for

> "custodia, qualem diligentissimus paterfamilias suis rebus adhibet"

in the usus vestimentorum, auri vel argenti, vel jumenti (*w*).

Our author only hurriedly touches upon the other grounds upon which obligations originate. That of Delict he turns over to the Criminal law. He designates those obligations as *quasi*-contracts,

Delict.

Quasi-contract.

> "quæ nec omnino ex pacto, nec omnino ex maleficio (oriuntur), sed tamen majorem cum pactis habent affinitatem, quam cum maleficiis;"

Quasi-delict.

and as *quasi*-delicts those,

> "quæ nec ad pacta accedunt, nec proprie ad maleficia, sed similiora sunt maleficiis quam pactis."

Bracton refers to the head of *quasi*-contract the negotiorum gestio, the tutela, the communio, the actio familiæ herciscundæ, the actio ex testamento and the condictio indebiti. Under the head of quasi-delict is placed the case, "si judex scienter male judicaverit," together with other transgressiones which are not specifically designated (*x*).

Bracton speaks of the extinction of obligations, as well per exceptionem, as *ipso jure*. Under the first head are mentioned the exceptions pactum de non petendo, exceptio doli, metus, rei judicatæ, jusjurandum, præscriptio. The extinction of obligations ipso jure, is stated to operate so that "nullæ remaneant ejus (sc. obligationis) reliquiæ." Under this latter head is mentioned solutio, which might be of two kinds *vera* and *imaginaria*. The obligation was extinguished by the *vera solutio* or actual payment,

Extinction of obligations.

(*w*) Bracton 62. 62 b. Fleta II. 59.
(*x*) Br. 99. 100 b. 101. 103.

(3) *Cf.* L. 4. pr. D. de pactis 2. 14. The English law of distress is compared with the Scotch law of the liability of the Invecta et Illata in Patterson's Compendium of English and Scotch law, 140.—*Tr.*

"quia soluto eo, quod debetur, omnis obligatio tollitur, sive ipse solvat, qui debeat, sive alius pro eo, sive debitore sciente, sive ignorante, et eo etiam invito" (from pr. J. quib. mod. 3. 29).

If payment was made on behalf of the principal debtor, it released the surety and vice versa. The *imaginaria solutio* was the acceptilatio:

"ut si dicatur: omne quod tibi debui ex quacunque causa, habesne acceptum? et respondeatur *vel scribatur*, habeo acceptumque fero" (*y*) (= § 1. J. l. c.)

Obligations were also extinguished ipso jure by novatio:

"ut, si *transfusa* sit obligatio de una persona in aliam, quæ in se susceperit obligationem; enim interventu novæ personæ, nova nascitur obligatio et prima tollitur, sicut de pecunia constituta, ut si quis in se susceperit alterius obligationem" (*cf.* § 3. J. l. c.) (*z*);

and also by *confusio*, which is explained in the following not very intelligible words:

"si confusa massa fuerit cum alia, ita quod non appareat."

Bracton besides lays down the following general rule similar to that in L. 153. D. de reg. juris 50. 17. (*aa*):

"quod eisdem modis dissolvitur obligatio, quæ nascitur ex contractu vel quasi, quibus contrahitur."

This he illustrates by the following application in detail:

"*re*, ut si res petenti restituatur; *verbis*, ut si fiat in contrarium......; *scripto*, ut si conscripserim me debere, scribat creditor se accepisse; *consensu*, ut si......ex utraque parte recedatur a contractu per communem dissensum utriusque et non alterius tantum; *traditione*, si res tradita retradatur; *junctura*, ut si fiat in contrarium" (*bb*).

(*y*) Br. 101. The "*scribatur*" is another proof of the views laid down in the beginning of this Chapter. *Cf.* Fleta II. 60. § 5–18.

(*z*) The "*transfusa*" in the definition of novatio is from L. 1. D. de novat. 46. 2. and Azo in Cod. de novat. f. 220. No. 4.

(*aa*) Fere quibuscunque modis obligamur, iisdem in contrarium actis liberamur.

(*bb*) Bracton 101. Fleta II. 60. §§ 19. 20.

This comparison recalls a similar one in the glossa ordin. ad L. 153. D. 50. 17. (*cc*).

(*cc*) Ex contractu quatuor modis obligamur: re, verbis, literis et consensu, sic et quatuor modis contrariis actis liberamur scilicet reddendo rem depositam, acceptilatione, item literis in contrarium missis ab eo, in quem priores expositæ fuerint; item contrario consensu etc.

CHAPTER XIX.

ACTIONS—PROCEDURE—PRACTICE.

Actions.

BRACTON'S notion of an action is taken from the Roman law:

> "actio nihil aliud est, quam jus prosequendi in judicio, quod alicui debetur" (pr. J. de act. 4. 6.) (*a*).

His division of actions is also Roman. His system of actions is constructed upon the basis furnished by Justinian's Institutes, and is not merely confined to the distinctions between placita criminalia and civilia, and petitory and possessory remedies, which are to be found in Glanville (*b*). Passing by less important divisions of actions, I dwell only on the following:

> "quod (actionum) quædam sunt *in rem*, quædam *in personam* et quædam *mixtæ*."

Actions in rem.

This division has obtained in the English law from Bracton's time until the present day. Actions in rem were, as in § 1. J. 4. 6., those

> "quæ dantur contra possidentem,......ut si quis petat ab alio rem certam......et contendat se habere jus, et inde esse dominum."

They were however confined to immovable things and rights, a consequence resulting from the bifurcation of the English law into two systems, one for immovables, and the other for movables. For movables there was no action in rem, no vindicatio, and damages only could be sued for, for

> "cum res sit mobilis......,placitum re vera erit in personam tantum" (*c*).

(*a*) 98 b. The accompanying explanation is taken from Azo f. 258 b No. 4.

(*b*) Glanville I. 1.; I. 3.

(*c*) Bracton 101 b. 102. 102 b. Fleta II. 60. § 21. Down to the present day no action in rem can be brought in England for movables. [This remark is *practically*

Actions in rem were, some petitory "*super proprietate et jure*," and some possessory "*super possessione ipsa* proditæ." Among the first Bracton enumerates: the rei vindicatio (breve de recto); the confessoria actio, "qua dicis tibi jus esse eundi," which was not designated by a special English name; and the negatoria actio, which was likewise known to the Eng-

---

true, and shows the author's accurate knowledge of the working of the English doctrine at home. But the remark perhaps is not in point of *doctrine* absolutely correct. The English action of replevin is a proceeding in which the title to any movables wrongfully *detained* might be tried and the actual possession of them recovered without reference to the question whether they had been wrongfully *taken*. In a case reported in 5 Adolphus & Ellis 142, Lord Chief Justice Denman said, "Every unlawful detention is a taking;" and in a case in 1 Siderfin 81, 82, it was decided that, in this action, the plea of non cepit infra sex annos was bad. The plea should have been either causa actionis non accrevit infra sex annos, or non cepit *nec detinuit* injuste etc. infra sex annos (and see 1 Keble 279, 317, 318, Gilbert on Replevin 131). Spelman in his Glossary defines the proceeding thus: Replegiare est rem apud alium *detentam*, cautione legitima interposita, redimere. This definition is quoted in the note to 1 Sch. & Lef. 327, where, in the text, Lord Redesdale says that Blackstone's definition of this action is too narrow, and that many old authorities will be found in the books for replevin being brought where there was no distress. In 1 Ball & Beaty 328, Lord Manners thought it a fair object of an action of replevin to try the title to goods under an alleged right of stoppage in transitu.

In Pennsylvania, Massachusetts, and elsewhere in the United States, this doctrine is carried out to the full practical extent of using the action of replevin as a remedy to change compulsorily the actual possession of movables in favor of any proprietor from whom they are, in any wise, wrongfully *detained*, without any reference to the question of a wrongful taking. This course of procedure is here considered as the practical effect of English doctrine as to the action. Property may be counterpleaded, or claimed by the defendant. In such a case, a bond or stipulation with surety, or a pecuniary deposit of the value, must be substituted pendente lite; and the original subject of the action may not be forthcoming to answer the plaintiff's ultimate recovery. This however is a universal and unavoidable incident of proceedings in rem as to movables.

But in England, for centuries there has perhaps not been any recourse to the action of replevin except for the immediate restoration of possession in the case of an actual wrongful taking. Such specific restoration does not contradict the general truth of the author's remark. In the action of detinue the possession is not changed pendente lite; and the plaintiff can only recover the goods, *or* their value. This, *in effect*, is a judgment for the value only. The rare and extraordinary cases in which specific possession of a chattel may be decreed by a court of equity, are so exceptional as to require no observation here, and do not conflict with the author's remark.—*Tr.*]

lish law. (1). Under the second head he places the following: the interdictum recuperandæ possessionis, which he calls *assisa novæ disseisinæ*, and which corresponds to the Roman interdict unde vi; the interdictum retinendæ possessionis, which falls also under the other category; and the interdictum adipiscendæ possessionis which he calls *assisa mortis antecessoris*, and also hereditatis petitio possessoria, as well as interdictum quorum bonorum (*d*). The relation of the possessory to the petitory actions was such that an appeal to the former did not preclude the subsequent use of the latter, while on the contrary the first use of petitory actions prevented all recourse from ever afterwards being had to the possessory. Hence where a petitory and a possessory action clashed, the causa possessionis was to be decided before the causa proprietatis, as in L. 5. § 1. D. ad leg. Jul. 48. 6., L. 3. C. de int. 8. 1., and c. 2. X. de caus. poss. 2. 12. (*e*).

Actions in personam.

Actions *in personam*, which following Azo our author also calls *nativæ**, were directed against the particular person liable,

> "cum aliquis teneatur ad aliquid dandum vel faciendum."

Actions in personam were divided, according to their origin, into civil actions, ex contractu vel quasi, and criminal (*i.e.* delict) actions, ex maleficio vel quasi. Of the latter kind, the actio furti, condictio furtiva, actio vi bonorum raptorum, legis Aquiliæ etc., are mentioned as examples. These were sometimes *pœnæ*, sometimes *rei*, and sometimes *rei et pœnæ persecutoriæ* (in this sense *mixtæ* as in § 16 *sq*. J. de act. 4. 6.), and were not transmitted to or against heirs quoad pœnam (*f*).

(*d*) Bracton 103.

(*e*) Bracton 104. 113. Quia esto, quod justiciarius prius de proprietate pronunciet,......si postea de possessione cognoscere voluerit inter eosdem, nihil ageret, quia placitum de recto utrumque jus determinat tam possessionis quam proprietatis, ut de Term. St. Trin. anno regni regis H. tertio in Com. Eborum. assisa mortis antecessoris, si Wilh. le Seneshall. Bracton 267. 283 b. 413.

* Azo 262. No. 7.: *Nativæ*, quia nascuntur ex contractibus etc., in opposition to *dativæ* quæ dantur ex legibus.

(*f*) Bracton 101 b. 102. 103 b. 104.

(1) *Cf.* L. 2. pr. D. si servitus vindicetur 8. 5.—*Tr.*

Actiones mixtæ, "tam in rem, quam in personam, quia mixtam habent causam ad utrumque," were the three Roman actions of partition, of which one, the familiæ herciscundæ, has already been referred to in Chapter XVI. In these quilibet actor et reus, but he was called actor "qui primus provocaverit ad judicium" (*g*).

Mixed actions.

Bracton does not treat of exceptions in connection with actions, but discusses them incidentally to the writ of right in a tract, specially devoted to them, entitled "de exceptionibus" (Lib. V. Tract. 5.) ([2]). Out of Bracton's ample exposition of the requisites and effects of the different exceptions, I advert only to the following points, which are connected with our present purpose. The definition,

Exceptions.

> "est autem exceptio *actionis elisio*, per quam actio perimitur aut differtur,"

recalls L. 2. pr. D. de exc. 44. 1. The division into exceptiones *peremptoriæ* and *dilatoriæ* herein indicated seems however to have retained no absolute character (*h*). Bracton, using a simile of Azo's, calls exceptions shields against the swords of actions (*i*), and the principle "qui excipit est quasi actor" held good so that the defendant had the onus probationis of his exception, just as the plaintiff had to prove his ground of action (*j*). To exceptions were opposed *replicationes* (the example mentioned in pr. J. de repl. 4. 14. being repeated), and to replicationes, triplicationes (no mention being made of duplicationes), etc.

(*g*) Bracton 102 b. 369 b. 372. 445 b. Fleta V. 9. §§ 1–4.

(*h*) Bracton 399 b. 187 b. [*Cf.* §§ 8–10 J. de excep. 4. 13.; L. 3. D. de except. præscrip. 44. 1. Reeves I. 451.—*Tr.*]

(*i*) Bracton 399 b. Et sicut actores armantur actionibus et quasi accinguntur gladiis, ita rei e contra muniuntur exceptionibus et defenduntur quasi clipeis. *Cf.* Azo 263 b. No. 6.

(*j*) Bracton 400. 215 b. 301 b.: qui excepit probare debet exceptionem.

([2]) This remark is based upon the author's analysis of Bracton's fifth book in Chapter II. In note ([2]) to that Chapter it has already been remarked that the fifth book is analyzed differently by Reeves, who applies the title breve de recto to its first tract only.—*Tr.*

Procedure.

Procedure offers but little for our purposes in Bracton. In its main features the development of that branch of the law had been so much upon the basis of peculiarly English views and principles, and, as far as actions in rem were concerned, so much in the forms and spirit of the feudal system, that the Roman law had not been able to exercise the same influence there as elsewhere, and has left in it but few and detached traces. On the other hand, however, a certain number of principles were transferred from the procedure of the Canon to that of the English law. This is not surprising, for both systems were coexistent in England, the Canonical procedure being practically used in the ecclesiastical courts. The Canon law influence is also seen in Bracton's discussion of the duties and office of judges. The judge, he declares, must be incorruptible: "abstineat omni munere." *Munus* is here taken in its widest sense, as expressed in c. 114. Caus. 1. qu. 1, and the penalties prescribed in L. 3. 6. C. ad leg. Jul. rep. 9. 27. are here explained as applicable (*k*). Moreover, the judge could be challenged as suspectus on account of the social relations mentioned in the Decretals (consanguinitas, amicitia, inimicitia, familiaritas etc.). The grounds of suspicion, laid down by the Canon law for excluding witnesses, were early considered as conclusive in England in challenging jurors. Glanville says:

> "excipi possunt *juratores eisdem modis, quibus et testes in Curia Christianitatis* juste repelluntur,"

and Bracton remarks:

> "eisdem enim modis amoventur a sacramento, quibus etiam testes amoventur a testimonio."

This is explained by the original position of jurors, which was that of witnesses, who were cognizant of the facts (*l*).

(*k*) Bracton 106 b. Munus a manu, quale est res corporalis, quæ præstatur: munus a lingua, quale est blandiens et adulatoria supplicatio;......munus ab obsequio, quale est servitium acceptum et impensum.

(*l*) Bracton 412. 185. Causes for challenge: amicitia, inimicitia (magna et non levis), familiaritas, potestas, infamia etc. *Cf.* Glanville II. 12.; Fleta IV. 8.

The Canon law distinction between judex ordinarius and judex delegatus, between jurisdictio ordinaria and delegata, is also recognized by Bracton. The delegated jurisdiction was especially considered to exist in the judices itinerantes, and some of the principles mentioned by Bracton in regard to their powers and authority remind us strongly of like rules relating to ecclesiastical delegates (*m*).

Ordinary and delegated jurisdiction.

In regard to jurisdiction, the Roman rule "actor sequitur forum rei" held good; in one passage only, do I find a *forum contractus* alluded to (*n*). Other expressions are undoubtedly taken from the Canon law procedure, such as: *intentio*, in Fleta *narratio* ([3]) (also: proponere, fundare intentionem), by which the plaintiff stated his grounds for the action; *responsio* for the defendant's answer etc. In one passage is mentioned the *litis contestatio*, which however has not here at all its canonical importance (*o*). The most accurate possible description of the thing which was the object of the action was required in accordance with L. 6. D. de rei vind. 6. 1.:

Jurisdiction.

Intentio, responsio.

Litis contestatio.

> "in qualibet actione, per quam petitur res corporalis designare oportet petentem, quæ et qualis sit res, quæ petitur (*p*);

in connection with the same authority, and with the direction of L. 9. C. de jud. 3. 1. that

> "judices inprimis oportet rei qualitatem plena inquisitione discutere etc.",

---

(*m*) Bracton 108 b. Extenditur eorum jurisdictio ad omnia, sine quibus causa terminari non potest. Delegatus non potest subdelegare etc.

(*n*) Bracton 401.: quia conveniendus, *ubi contraxit* ille, qui contraxit.

(*o*) Bracton 373.: *usque ad litis contestationem, scilicet quousque fuerit præcise responsum intentioni petentis*; evidently after c. un. X. de litisc. 2. 5.

(*p*) Bracton 431 b. Si res mobilis petatur, oportet designare, utrum petatur animal vel vestis,......si vestis, utrum bombicina vel lana, vel de linio; si petatur res, quæ in pondere consistat,......tunc scire oportet cujus sit ponderis et cujus generis;......si autem quæ consistit in mensura, tunc utrum liquidum aut solidum;......de numero autem oportebit constare, quot modia, vel hujusmodi etc.

([3]) Bracton 240, uses the term narratio.—*Tr.*

should be placed the interrogation of the parties which Bracton enjoins upon the judges (*q*). I will not decide whether or not, the putting of the plaintiff into the possession of the disputed thing, in consequence of the persistent default of the defendant in an action in rem, is to be connected with the *missio in possessionem rei servandæ causa* occurring in like case in the Canon law procedure (c. 4. X. de dol. 2. 14.; c. 1. X. de eo, qui. 2. 15.): there may be here presented only an accidental external resemblance between legal principles of independent growth. It is to be remarked, however, that in one passage Bracton does not hesitate to speak of such putting into possession as *missio in seisinam quasi ex secundo decreto* (*r*).

Interrogations.

Some foreign principles are also to be found in the English law of Bracton's day relative to proof by charters. Bracton declares that a charta privata was evidence *against* but not *for* him by whom it was made:

Proof by charters.

> "facit aliquando quis scripturam *sibi* ipsi et tali scripturæ *non erit fides adhibenda;* aliquando facit *contra se,* et *tali scripturæ adhibetur fides.*"

He confines the liability to produce charters in court to instrumenta communia, in accordance with c. 12. X. de fide inst. 2. 22. He expressly lays down that charters need not be produced

> "*ad fundandam intentionem* cum non teneatur armare adversarium suum contra se,"

as in L. 7. C. de testib. 4. 20. and c. 3. § 35. Caus. 4. qu. 4. (*s*). The proof of the genuineness or authenticity of charters might be made per testes, i.e. by witnesses of their execution. Two of such witnesses agreeing made "*plenam probationem*" according to the rule, "in ore duorum vel trium testium stat omne verbum," while the evidence of one afforded only *semiplenam probationem*, "quæ in-

Probate of charters.

(*q*) Bracton 183 b. Bracton remarks that these interrogationes were not attended to by all judges. *Cf.* Fleta IV. 7. [*Cf.* Bracton 144, and cases in Rot. Cur. Reg. I. 30, 31, II. 78.—*Tr.*]

(*r*) Bracton 367.

(*s*) Bracton 33 b. 34. [*Cf.* cases in Rot. Cur. Reg. II. 73, 88, 99.—*Tr.*]

ducit præsumtionem." Where the witnesses contradicted each other,

> "si impares fuerint numeri......,majori et digniori parti standum erit;"

but if they were equal in numbers and dignity, the charter was held to be genuine,—principles, which if they do not entirely agree with those expressed in L. 3. § 2. L. 21. § 3. D. de test. 22. 5. and in c. 32. X. de test. 2. 20, may yet have derived their origin therefrom (*t*). Charters might also be proved by a comparison of seals, "*per collationem signorum.*" This mode of verification originated from the circumstance that the English law (even in the Saxon period) considered an essential requisite of the validity of a charter to be the seal, and not the signature of its maker. It hence held the authenticity of the seal to be sufficient proof of the authenticity of the charter (*u*). It can hardly be doubted that this collatio signorum (which was also known to Glanville) must be traced back to the Roman comparison of handwriting, although the details of the Roman proceeding were not copied (*v*).

Seals.

The authenticity or original genuineness of a charter is very clearly distinguished by Bracton from its credibility and from its value as evidence. Where a charter presented erasures, cancellings and the like, especially if they occurred in loco suspecto (*w*), its credibility was impaired if not wholly destroyed; for

Exceptions to charters.

> "calumniosam scripturam vim in judicio obtinere non convenit" (from L. 2. D. de fid. instr. 22. 4.).

(*t*) Bracton 38. 396–398. Azo f. 85. No. 1.

(*u*) Reeves I. 88. [See also Hardy in Rot. Chart. in Tur. Lond. pp. xxxiv *sq.*; Attorney Gen. *v.* Hospital of St. John, Jurist, N. S , vol. X. 896.—*Tr.*]

(*v*) Bracton 398 b.:—si conferant alia sigilla, quæ aliquando in judicio approbata fuerint,......et si omnibus modis conveniant,......ita quod nulla in eis appareat differentia, hoc solum sufficit ad probationem chartæ. *Cf.* Glanv. X. 12.; Fleta VI. 33. 34.

(*w*) Bracton, ibid. The addition of "loco suspecto scilicet *in narratione facti,*" seems to be founded upon a misunderstanding of c. 3. X. de fid. inst. 2. 22. where in the words: "et literæ in narratione facti si erratum sit, possunt incunctanter abradi," the contrary is said.

Certain exceptions to the legal validity of a charter might destroy its value as evidence, although the writing and seal were admitted. From the foregoing, it will be seen how the English law had been developed by contact with the Roman since Glanville's time. Glanville lays it down as an axiom that a man could not object to a charter the seal of which he acknowledged to be his own, even when his type seal had been improperly or fraudulently used:

> "nam suæ malæ custodiæ imputatur, si damnum incurret per sigillum suum male custoditum."

Bracton, on the contrary, unhesitatingly admits the exceptions doli, metus, erroris etc., and in doing so undoubtedly shows the influence of the Roman law (x).

(x) Glanville X. 12. Bracton 396–398. [*Qu:* if there be any difference between these authors, except in the respective applications of their propositions?—*Tr.*]

CHAPTER XX.

ASSISA NOVÆ DISSEISINÆ.

Importance of this assise.

ONLY *one* of the English legal remedies discussed by Bracton demands our particular attention, viz. the assisa (recognitio) novæ disseisinæ. This assise was the action to remedy disseisin, i.e. where a man, actually seized, was deprived of, or obstructed in his possession. It excites attention not merely for its importance in regard to the history of the trial by jury, but also because it is just here that the influence of the Roman law shows itself.

Its origin.

The assisa novæ disseisinæ corresponds to the interdicts unde vi and uti possidetis of the Roman law (1), and still more strikingly to the *remedium spoliationis* of the then Canon law. It is in fact often designated by the latter name in the older English authorities. It did not originate in the general customary law, but owed its introduction to an act of legislation. This circumstance is what Glanville refers to in expressions such as:

> "ex beneficio constitutionis regiæ,"
>
> "disseisito *hujus constitutionis* beneficio subvenitur."

Bracton also alludes to this legislative introduction, when he says:

> "de beneficio principis ei succurritur per assisam novæ disseisinæ, *multis vigiliis excogitatam et inventam*" (*a*).

In fact the first mention of this legal remedy can be shown to be in an act of legislation of 1176, the Assises of North-

---

(*a*) Glanville XIII. 1. 32. Bracton 164 b.

---

(1) See Spence I. 220.—*Tr.*

ampton, by which the Constitutions of Clarendon were revised (*b*). It is there said in Article X.:

> "justiciæ domini regis faciant fieri recognitionem de disseisinis factis super assisam.

It is not impossible that our assise derives its existence from the Assises of Northampton, if not from the Constitutions of Clarendon, both of which have unfortunately come down to us incomplete. There was previously known to the English law no special remedy to protect possession against disseisin. When therefore the want of such protection and the need of a speedy relief for such wrongs came to be felt (*c*), the legislative authority, especially if it was advised by judges and ecclesiastics of Civilian training, found its most convenient models to be the Roman possessory actions, which were then most extensively used in the actual practice of the courts Christian (*d*). This source, when once opened, was the more readily applied to, since, as we have seen in Chapter XI, the English lawyers had adopted the general features of the then standard Roman theory of possession. In its details, this will be shown in what follows.

Like the interdict unde vi, the assisa novæ disseisinæ served only to protect the possession of immovables, including the quasi-possession of *servitutes* etc. (*e*). Movables were, indeed, excluded from the application of possessory as well as petitory remedies. Among movables were reckoned ships, as in L. 1. § 7. D. de vi 43. 16.,

Applied to immovables.

> "item non competit ei, qui *de nave* ejectus fuerit......, non magis, quam si tractus esset de equo suo sive de vehiculo, curru vel carecta;"

but not wooden houses in solo proprio, "sive cohærent, sive non" (*cf.* L. 1. § 8. D. l. c.) (*f*).

(*b*) Printed in Phillips, Engl. Rechtsgesch. III. 53. under the title: Assisæ Henrici regis factæ apud Clarendon et consecratæ apud Northamptune. [See Wilkins, 330; Palgrave's Commonwealth, Vol. I., Part II., p. clxviii.—*Tr.*]

(*c*) Bracton 164 b.: per summariam cognitionem absque magna juris solennitate.

(*d*) The words "multis vigiliis excogitatam et inventam" in the above quoted passage, would perhaps augur a more scientific preparation.

(*e*) In servitutes it had other names, e.g. assisa de communia etc. Bracton 224 *sq.* 164 b. [But *cf.* Reeves I. 345.—*Tr.*]

(*f*) Bracton 168.

Disseisin.

The action presupposed the occurrence of a previous *disseisin.* But the notion of disseisin was not limited to the strict meaning of the word, to forcible putting out of possession, which Bracton calls *ejectio*, *dejectio*, or disseisina violenta. Disseisin, like the Canonical spoliatio (which expression is not seldom used for disseisin in the older English sources), included also what Bracton styles disseisina simplex. Disseisina simplex comprised every case where the actual possessor was deprived of, or obstructed in his possession without the disseisor making use of force. Disseisina violenta, might or might not be attended with vis armata (*g*). As in the Roman law, it also occurred in the case in which the possessor was deprived of his liberty while continuing to be still on the land itself, and in that in which his return and resumption of possession after absence were forcibly prevented.

> Bracton 166 b. "Sed si quis meos et me dejecerit, et quosdam retinuerit et vinxerit......,competit mihi assisa; desii enim possidere, cum servi mei vel alii, per quos retinui possessionem, ab alio possidentur...... Item si ego dejectus non fuero, *in possessione tamen vinctus sum* ......,adhuc competit mihi assisa" (*cf.* L. 1. §§ 46. 47. D. de vi. 43. 16.);

and

> f. 161 b.: "fit disseisina, cum quis ad *nundinas vel peregre profectus fuerit*, nemine in domo relicto......,alius in possessionem ingrediatur *et ipsum reversum non admittat*, vel cum ingredi voluerit, per se vel assumptis viribus violenter repellat" (from L. 1. § 24. 25. D. l. c.; L. 6. § 1.; L. 7. D. de acq. poss. 41. 2.).

Simple disseisin.

Disseisina simplex occurred not merely in cases of corporal obstruction of possession, or of usurping and exceeding servitutes, but also in that of unjustly contesting the rights of the possessor:

(*g*) Bracton 162 b.: *telorum* appellatione omnia, in quibus singuli homines nocere possunt, accipiuntur; sed si quis venerit sine armis et ipsa concertatione tigna sumpserit, fustes et lapides, talis dicitur *vis armata.* Si quis autem venerit cum armis, armis ad dejiciendum non usus fuerit et dejecerit, vis armata dicitur esse facta; sufficit enim terror armorum, ut videatur armis dejecisse etc. Nearly verbatim from L. 3. §§ 2–11. D. de vi. 43. 16.—*Cf.* Fleta IV. 4.

"cum commodum utendi ei omnino auferat quominus commode......uti possit impediat, possessionem inquietando vel perturbando...... Etiam si quis......uti voluerit in alterius tenemento......arando, contendendo tenementum esse suum quod est alterius" (*h*).

It also happened in cases where a man injuriously interfered with another's legal rights by things done on his own land, cases to which according to the Roman law the possessory inderdicts did not apply, but other legal remedies (e.g. operis novi nunciatio, int. quod vi aut clam) (*i*). Finally Bracton expressly states that disseisin might occur in certain cases where one was wrongfully put out of possession through a wrongful judgment or execution; a principle whose origin was probably derived from the Roman law (*j*).

Self-defence against an attempt to disseise.

As in the Roman law it was proper for a person first to resort to self-defence with moderamen inculpatæ tutelæ, when an attempt was made to put him out of possession.

"Incontinenti vim vi repellere (licet)". "Unde...... licitum erit, cum armis contra pacem venientem ut expellat, cum armis repellere,......sed tamen *cum talis discretionis moderamine, quod injuriam non committat*" (*k*).

After disseisin had actually taken place the disseisee was permitted to right himself immediately and retake possession, for he was considered to lose at first only the natural and not the civil possession (see Chapter XI.):

Ejection of disseisor as a remedy.

"— quod ille, qui ita disseisitus fuit, per se, si possit, vel sumtis viribus et resumtis, dum tamen *sine aliquo*

(*h*) Bracton 216 b. 161 b.:—ut si quis voluerit in alterius tenemento contra ipsius tenentis voluntatem arando, fodiendo, falcando,......vel pecora immittendo vel alio quocumque modo sic servitutem imponendo = L. 3. §§ 2. *sq.* D. uti poss. 43. 17.; L. 11. D. de vi 43. 16.—Upon disseisin in its relation to servitutes: Bracton 221 *sq.*

(*i*) These were called *nocumenta* injuriosa, for which an assisa nov. diss., might be brought, and in cases where that did not suffice, a special assisa de nocumentis. Bracton 231 b.–235. Fleta IV. 26–28. [But *cf.* Reeves I. 345.—*Tr.*]

(*j*) Bracton 205. 205 b. *Cf.* c. 7. X. de rest. spol. 2. 13., and Bruns, Recht des Besitzes, 208 *sq.* [*Cf.* Reeves I. 321.—*Tr.*]

(*k*) Br. 162 b. 163. = L. 1. § 27., L. 3. § 9. D. de vi 43. 16.; L. 1. C. unde vi 8. 4.

> *intervallo, flagrante disseisina* et maleficio, rejiciat spoliantem."

In this latter case the ejected disseisor had not the remedy of the assise (*l*). If however the original disseisee had not incontinenti made a successful use of his right of self-redress, if he had, as Bracton viewed it, lost both the natural and the civil possession "per impotentiam, negligentiam" etc., his only remedy left was then the assise. For, just as strictly as the constitution of Valentinian, L. 7. C. unde vi 8. 4., forbade taking the law into one's own hands except in the case just mentioned, the English law prohibited doing so. From Bracton's remarks there is little doubt that the Law just cited was regarded as the authority for that principle (*m*).

The following points also present themselves for our consideration in this assise. He who had possession *proprio nomine* could alone be plaintiff, as in the law of the Digest. Hence he who *alieno nomine possidet* could not be plaintiff (the rule being that his ejection was to be remedied by the proper possessor's bringing the assise):

Plaintiff and defendant in the assise.

> "pertinet tantum ad eos querela, qui nomine suo proprio tenementum tenent, et non alieno".— "Nulli autem competit querela nec remedium per assisam, qui in possessione fuerit nomine alieno, quia talis non

---

(*l*) Bracton 163. 164 b. = L. 3. § 9. D. de vi. The following corresponds to the case given in L. 17. l. c. Ejicio te, tu me incontinenti et flagrante disseisina, non recuperabo per assisam, quia passus sum id quod feci. Item ejicio te, et tu me, et ego te postea incontinenti iterum, adhuc competit tibi assisa......et ita erit in infinitum, quod verus possessor ejicere poterit incontinenti, et non competit contra ipsum assisa, et si ipse a spoliatore ejiceretur......poterit spoliatorem rejicere, et non competit spoliatori assisa; 163 b. *Cf.* Fleta IV. 2.

(*m*) Bracton 163 b. Si forte assisam contemnat et possessionem suam sibi usurpare præsumat, competit spoliatori......assisa, non quia injuste disseisitus sit, sed quia sine judicio et quia per negligentiam veri domini utramque habere incepit possessionem, naturalem et civilem. Bracton 210 b.; Si ad verum dominum violenter possessio pervenerit......et ubi conqueri deberet, facit se judicem et ejicit disseisitorem......, disseisitor indistincte......possessionis commodum reportabit...... Pœna autem erit spoliatoris, ut si sua sit res.......*quod illam spoliator restituat cum fructibus......: vix tamen super proprietatem in posterum audiendus* (mitigation of L. 7. C. unde vi?). *Cf.* c. 11. X. de rest. spol. 2. 13.

> possidet, licet in possessione fuerit, sed ipse possidet, cujus nomine possidetur" (*n*).

The result did not depend upon the right of possession, whether it had been a possessio justa or injusta. For, as Bracton often repeats:

> "*ille, qui possidet, licet jus non habeat, eo tamen, quod in possessione est, plus juris habet propter seisinam, quam ille, qui est extra possessionem.*"

The action was hence maintainable by the possessor bonæ fidei, as well as malæ fidei, and even by the disseisor himself contra quemcunque tertium (*o*). As in the Roman law the action was maintainable against the spoliator himself on the ground either of actual perpetration, or of instigation (besides that of ratihabitio); against the master in respect to his familia; and against all participants in the disseisin.

> "Item incidit in assisam non solum ille, qui facit nomine alieno, verum etiam ille, cujus nomine fit, dum tamen factum suorum et injuriam advocaverit" (*p*).

Heirs were liable only *quoad restitutionem*, not *quoad pœnam*. Secondary possessors were liable to the assise when the land was acquired as *litigiosa*, or only as *vitiosa*, an effect of the decree of the Lateran Council of 1216, and c. 18. X. de rest. spol. 2. 13. (*q*).

The object of the assise (independently of the public penalty) was the restitution of the land cum fructibus:

Object of the assise.

> "res ipsa cum fructibus omnibus medio tempore perceptis scilicet a tempore disseisinæ usque ad judicium perceptis et percipiendis" (*cf.* L. 1. § 40. D. de vi),

together with full damages and an accounting for and restitution of all movables which had been upon the land:

(*n*) Bracton 165. 167 b. 168. 206.: nec competit assisa alicui, nisi ei tantum, qui tunc, quum ejiceretur, possidebat, nec alius ejici visus est, quam is, qui possidet nomine proprio vel alieno = L. 1. §§ 9. 23. D. de vi. Fleta IV. 3. § 1. *sq.*

(*o*) Bracton 165. 166 b. 184. 184 b. 196. = L. 2. D. uti poss. 43. 17.; L. 128. D. de reg. jur. 50. 17.

(*p*) Bracton 171. 171 b. where L. 1. §§ 12–18. D. de vi are partially given verbatim. Bracton 174 b. 204 b. [*Cf.* Reeves I. 324, 325.—*Tr.*]

(*q*) Bracton 171. 204.: videndum erit, utrum illam habeat *vitiosam*. 204 b.

> "habenda erit ratio rerum ablatarum, quæ cum ipsa re restituantur......, non solum, quæ propriæ fuerunt ipsius disseisiti, verum etiam omnes illæ, quæ apud illum depositæ commodatæ......fuerunt,......quia hæc omnia sub habendi verbo continentur."

Bracton thus merely repeats L. 1. §§ 32 to 39. D. de vi (*r*).

(*r*) Bracton 186 b. 187.

CHAPTER XXI.

CRIMINAL LAW.

English Criminal law.

Influence of the Roman law thereupon.

THE English Criminal law as we find it in Bracton's tract on the Crown, also, shows marks of the contact with the Roman law. The Church and the Canon law had, however, a greater influence upon its development, but it would exceed the limits of the present investigation for me to go into a connected and detailed examination of the influence of those high authorities for the penal law doctrine of the middle ages (*a*). I shall therefore confine myself to what is contained in the following paragraphs.

Punishments, crimes.

A perfected theory of penal law cannot be expected from Bracton, if we consider the then state of legal science; we only meet with some general principles concerning criminal penalties and the punishment of crime, which are taken from the Title of the Digest de pœnis. Thus he enumerates the different kinds of punishments according to L. 6. § 2. L. 7. L. 8. pr. *sq.* D. de pœn. 48. 19.:

> "sunt autem quædam, quæ adimunt vitam vel membra. Sunt autem, quæ auferunt civitatem, *burgum* vel provinciam,......quæ continent exilium perpetuum vel ad tempus, vel corporis coertionem, scilicet *imprisonamentum*...... Sunt quædam, quæ fustigationem, verberationem, *pœnam pilloralem*......et damnum cum infamia inducunt. Sunt etiam quædam, quæ dignitatis et ordinis depositionem inducunt, vel alicujus actus privationem vel prohibitionem."

His injunction to the judges to inflict a mild or a severe

(*a*) Biener has touched upon much which relates thereto, in his History of Inquisitorial Procedure and in his work upon the English Jury.

punishment according to the different character of particular cases is taken from L. 11. D. de pœnis:

> "—respiciendum est judicanti, ne quid aut durius aut remissius constituatur, quam causa deposcit; nec enim aut severitatis aut clementiæ gloria affectanda est, sed perpenso judicio prout quæque res expostulat statuendum est...... Et pœnæ potius molliendæ sunt, quam exasperandæ."

From the same source, viz., L. 16. D. de pœnis, is derived also the following passage in Bracton:

> "*Facta* puniuntur, ut furta, homicidia; *scripta*, ut falsa et libelli famosi; *consilia*, ut conjurationes. Sed hæc quatuor genera, consideranda sunt septem modis...... *Causa*, ut in verberibus etc. (as in L. 16. § 2. D. de pœn.). *Persona* dupliciter spectatur sc. ejus, qui fecit, et ejus, qui passus est, aliter enim puniuntur ex iisdem factionibus (sic!) servi quam liberi, et aliter, qui quid in dominum parentemve commiserit, quam in extraneum;...... et similiter ætatis ratio habenda est. *Tempus* discernit prædonem a fure, vel effractorem, et furem diurnum a nocturno. *Quantitas* discernit furem ab abigeo......, ut si quis suem surripuerit, fur erit, et si quis gregem, abigeus erit. *Eventus*, ut si ex voluntate et conscientia certa fecerit quis aliquid......an ex eventu......: et secundum hoc aut erit felonia aut infortunium" (*b*).

From the Roman law are derived a series of provisions relative to the outlawry, *utlagatio*, of a fugitive criminal. Bracton cites different passages of the Code and Digest in confirmation of the consequent confiscation of property, of the prohibition to harbor and the permission to slay an outlaw, and places outlawry altogether upon the same footing as the Roman capitis diminutio maxima in regard to its effects and consequences (*c*).

Outlawry.

(*b*) Bracton 104 b. 105. We also find here L. 11. § 2. D. de pœn. Delinquunt latrones proposito per factionem; ebrii impetu per ebrietatem, cum ad manus vel ferrum pervenitur; casu, cum per infortunium, ut si aliquis venando per telum in feram missum hominem interfecerit.

(*c*) Bracton 125. 128 b. 129. Here he cites L. 1. C. 9. 39.; L. 2. C. 9. 40.; L. 3. § 6. D. 48. 8.; L. ult. D. 48. 17.

In regard to the particular crimes themselves there is little to remark. The *crimen læsæ majestatis* takes not merely its name, but also its definition, from the Roman law:

Crimen læsæ majestatis.

> "si quis ausu temerario machinatus sit in mortem domini regis, vel aliquid egerit vel agi procuraverit ad seditionem......exercitus sui, vel procurantibus auxilium et consilium præbuerit vel consensum."

We also find the confiscation of the traitor's property and the incapacity of his issue to inherit, unmistakably connected with L. 5. C. ad leg. Jul. maj. 9. 8:

> "*heredum suorum perpetua exheredatione*,......est enim tam grave crimen istud, ut vix permittitur heredibus, quod vivant" (*d*).—

Furtum.

So also we meet with the definition of furtum,

> "*furtum est secundum leges contrectatio rei alienæ fraudulenta cum animo furandi* invito illo domino, cujus res illa fuerit,"

which the Roman law has made current with us; but the distinction between furtum manifestum and nec manifestum connected therewith has nothing to do with the same distinction in the Roman law, but rests alone upon specially English ideas (*e*). Finally, what Bracton says concerning *injuria* is nothing but an extract from the corresponding title of the Institutes (IV. 4.). He discriminates between injuria arising from words, and that arising from acts done (*Verbal und Realinjurie*):

> "fit autem injuria non solum, cum quis pugno percussus fuerit, verberatus, vulneratus, vel fustibus cæsus, verum cum ei convicium dictum fuerit, vel de eo factum carmen famosum" (§ 1. J. de inj. 4. 4.);

and between injuria levis et atrox; the latter being estimated

> "ex ipso facto, ut si quis fuerit male vulneratus......et male tractatus contra pacem regis; item ex loco, si in curia dom. regis, si coram justiciariis......,in nundinis, in foro, vel alibi coram omni populo; item locus vul-

---

(*d*) Bracton 118 b. Glanville XII. 1.: rebus insuper suis omnibus confiscandis et *heredibus suis in perpetuum exheredandis*. *Cf.* Fleta I. 21. § 1.

(*e*) Bracton 150 b. Fleta I. 36. § 1.

neris......ut si in fronte vel in oculo magis quam in loco secreto etc." (*cf.* § J. l. c.)

Injuria could also be inflicted upon a man in the persons of those belonging to his household or family:

Injuria.

"patitur injuriam quis non solum per se ipsum sed etiam per alios, quos habet in potestate, sicut per liberos......et uxorem......servientes et servos, si pulsati fuerint et verberati in contumeliam suam, vel quatenus sua interfuit operibus eorum non caruisse" (§ 2. 3. J. l. c.).

The amount of the pœna was to be regulated by the judge "secundum qualitatem delicti et personæ," but after a lapse of time the injured party lost his right to recover it, per dissimulationem, for he was then held to have pardoned the wrong done him (*f*).

Some of the propositions laid down concerning homicide are also undoubtedly of Canonical origin. The distinction that the deed might be perpetrated

Homicide.

"*lingua* vel *facto;* lingua tribus modis: præcepto, consilio, defensione sive tuitione; facto quatuor modis: justitia, necessitate, casu et voluntate,"

belongs to the ecclesiastical theory, and is found almost identically in c. 2. X. de cler. pug. 5. 14.:

"homicidium autem tam facto, quam præcepto sive consilio aut defensione non est dubium perpetrari."

Necessitas only excused according to Bracton when it was inevitabilis, i.e. when, as in c. 2. X. de hom. 5. 12., the fatal blow had been inflicted

"sine odii meditatione *in metu et dolore animi* se et suos liberando."

—In casual homicide (most of the examples of which are taken from the Title X. de hom. 5. 12.) (*g*) the decisive question was:

(*f*) Bracton 155. 155 b. Fleta II. 1. §§ 2–9. [*Cf.* Reeves II. 45.—*Tr.*]

(*g*) Bracton 120 b. 121. 136 b. e.g.: ut si magister causa disciplinæ discipulum verberat = c. 7. 12. X. de homic.; vel si quis deponebat fœnum de curru = c. 14. l. c.; vel si cum socius luderet cum socio, et jocosa levitate percusserit = c. 8. 9. l. c.

"utrum quis dederit *operam rei licitæ vel illicitæ,*"

as in c. 49. 51. dist. 50., c. 9. 13. 23. 25. X. de hom. 5. 12. In the first case only, and in that alone when necessary diligence had been used, was the act excusable (*h*). The following passage lays down that all participants in the act were to be punished for homicide:

> "omnes dici possunt homicidæ, et illi, qui percusserunt, et illi qui tenuerunt malo animo, dum percussus fuerit; item et illi, qui voluntate occidendi venerunt, licet non percusserint; item et illi,......qui venerunt, ut præstarent consilium et auxilium occisoribus, quamvis aliquando eorum violentia repellatur; item......(tenetur) et ille, qui præcipit percutere et occidere, quia cum non sint immunes a culpa, immunes esse non debent a pœna."

This passage corresponds throughout to the principles which are laid down in the Decretal of Alexander III., c. 6. X. de homic., issued upon the occasion of the death of Archbishop Becket (*i*). Finally, Bracton speaks of suicide (*j*), and distinguishes, after L. 3. D. de bonis eor. 48. 21, whether it had been committed after apprehension in the act of crime, or in order to escape sentence, or whether it was done tædio vitæ vel impatientia doloris alicujus; in the two first cases the confiscation of all the suicide's property took place (*k*).

(*h*) Bracton l. c.

(*i*) Bracton 121. Fleta I. 23. *Cf.* with the passage given above, the text of the decretal: § 2. Illi etiam, qui non, ut ferirent, sed ut percussoribus opem ferrent, si forte per aliorum violentiam impedirentur...... § 4. Hi quoque non sunt a culpa liberi, nec a pœna debent esse immunes etc.

(*j*) "Si quis fecerit *feloniam de se ipso.*"

(*k*) Bracton 130. 150.

APPENDIX.

APPENDIX.

Translator's Note to Chapter VII., pp. 73, 74.

It was originally intended that this note should be devoted to the consideration of Bracton's influence upon the English law from his own day to the present, and to a discussion of his authority during the period of the Year Books and in modern times. After mature consideration, however, the translator has felt himself compelled to abandon this purpose. A closer examination of this interesting subject showed it to be impossible that justice could be done to the influence which Bracton's writings have exercised during so long a period without going into a thorough and systematic historical investigation. The cases and authorities to be commented upon are so numerous, the researches requisite are so extensive, that an elaborate discussion of much length would have been indispensable. Bracton's great work must indubitably be considered an historical phenomenon in European jurisprudence, in some respects without a parallel. The appearance of a treatise of such magnitude, exhaustiveness, and original power, seems, indeed, to have been the true birth of a scientific jurisprudence in England, the successful development of which has steadily progressed to the present day. To trace the influence of the great jurist in whose writings that development originated, is a subject of such extensive range and fundamental importance as perhaps to require a book of itself. Certain it is, that no attempt to do justice to the illustrious father of the Common law could be compressed within the modest limits of this translation.

This determination has necessarily involved the omission of a translation of Dr. Biener's pages upon the authority of Bracton during the period of the Year Books. Dr. Biener's interpretation of those authorities and his applications of that interpretation differ so much with the views entertained by the translator, that the latter felt unwilling to reproduce them without commentary, a task which could not properly be performed without going into a discussion of the whole subject of Bracton's influence.

TRANSLATOR'S NOTE TO CHAPTER XV., P. 124.

According to Bracton, a right which was a *servitus* of the servient tenement, was a *libertas* of the dominant tenement. F. 220 b.: jura autem sive *libertates* dici poterit ratione tenementorum *quibus debentur. Servitutes* vero ratione tenementorum *a quibus debentur*, et semper consistunt in alieno et non in proprio, quia nemini servire potest suus fundus proprius, et nullus hujusmodi servitutes constituere potest, nisi ille qui fundum habet et tenementum, quia praediorum aliud liberum, aliud servituti suppositum. *Liberum dici poterit quod in nullo tenetur vel astringitur praediis vicinorum.* Si autem teneatur, dicitur servituti suppositum quod prius fuerat liberum. *Libertates* has therefore here a signification similar to that given by Houard to the word *aisiamenta* in the writ in Glanville, XII. 14. That writer remarks in his note to Glanville (Traités sur les Coutumes Anglo-Normandes, I. 548) : Sous cette dénomination (*aisiamenta*) sont comprises toutes les servitudes prédiales, dont on jouit sur les fonds d'autrui. Reeves, I. 174, translates Glanville's term *aisiamenta* by the word *easements*, and in commenting (ib. 344, 345) on Bracton, f. 231, says also: "The writ in Glanville (XII. 14) to the sheriff, commanding that precipias R. quod, etc., permittat H. *aisiamenta* sua, etc., was preserved with some small differences of form. He was directed that justicies R. quod, etc., permittat H. habere rationabile *estoverium*, etc., as the case might be, of wood, turbary and the like." It is important to observe that Bracton does not here use the word *aisiamenta.* This fact, together with his definition of the word libertates above given, may lead us to infer that he may have here purposely avoided using the word *aisiamenta.* If such be the case, the circumstance is historically interesting in its bearing upon the development of the existing doctrine relative to the distinction since established between a *profit à prendre* and an *easement.* (See 7 Mees. & Wel. 63, 69, 77–79, 4 El. & Bl. 702, 704, 711.)

TRANSLATOR'S NOTE TO CHAPTER XVIII., PP. 141, 142.

In Coggs *v.* Bernard, 2 Ld. Raym. 915, 916, Holt, C. J., cites this passage thus: Sed magna differentia est inter mutuum et commodatum; quia is qui rem MUTUAM accepit ad ipsam restituendam tenetur vel ejus pretium si forte incendio, ruina, naufragio, aut latronum vel hostium incursu, consumta fuerit, vel deperdita, substracta vel ablata, etc. Jones (Law of Bailments, 64 x.) points out that in this reading *mutuam* is substituted for *commodatam*, and adds: "But what can then be made of the words 'ad *ipsam* restituendam?' There is certainly some mistake in the passage, which must be very ancient, for the oldest manuscript that I have seen is conformable to Tottel's edition. I suspect the omission of a whole line after the word pretium, where the manuscript has a full point; and possibly the sentence omitted may be thus supplied from Justinian, whom Bracton copied: 'At is, qui *mutuum* accepit, obligatus remanet, si forte incendio, etc.'" Sir W. Jones, Chief Justice Holt, and Dr. Güterbock, each, therefore, suggest different emendations.

INDEX.

F.

G.

H.

I.

J.

K.

L.

M.

N.

O.

P.

Q.

R.

S.

T.

U.

V.

W.

Y.

ERRATA.

Page 22 note (*b*) l. ult. for *Dudg.* read *Dugd.*
p. 37 note (*p*) l. 4, after *resembling* insert *in some respects.*
p. 40 note (*c*) l. 4, for *legis* read *leges.*
p. 51 note (*e*) l. ult. for 43, 21 read 43. 21.
p. 53 note (*j*) l. 4, for *incorporeales* read *incorporales.*
p. 119 l. 24, for *exedit* read *excedit.*
p. 122 l. 1, and inset note, for *incorporeales* read *incorporales.*
p. 158 note (*x*) l. 2, for *hese* read *these.*

MSS of Bracton

Brit Mus –

Harl . 653
– 656
– 763
– 817
– 1242
– 3416
– 3422

Addit. 11353 from Libr. of Sir Thomas Crewe Kt Kings Serjt to James I 1624
– 21614 from Glastonbury Abbey
– 24067 from Chertsey Abbey

Royal 9 E. XIV . p. 174

Lincoln's Inn

~~Maynard~~ Hale CXVI (CXXXV) Selden's ?

~~Noblemen~~ Anon XI (CXXXVI) from Ranulph Cholmeley Serjt at law 1563

Grays Inn 21 from Serjt Godbold 1653

Middle Temple 1

Camb. Univ. Libr.

414. Dd. VII 6 . Art. 79
422 Dd. VII. 14. Art 7
1021 Ee. IV. 4
890 Ee . I . 1

Queens Coll no 23

Oxford –

Bodleian Libr.
Bodley MS. 2346 . 2407 in Catal. AD 1697
Tanner MS. 189

Merton Coll. CCCXX

York Minster 49
Worcester Cathedral 87
~~647~~

~~[illegible] 284~~

Lambeth – 92
" – 93

Middlehill Sir T Phillipps 136
Stowe CLXV sold 1849 to Earl of Ashburnham

5.0

Stanford Court
Sir T. Winnington

Longleat
Marquess of Bath

www.ingramcontent.com/pod-product-compliance
Lightning Source LLC
LaVergne TN
LVHW011228110826
845150LV00006B/1573

* 9 7 8 1 4 2 5 5 1 5 2 9 4 *